THE DIRTY DOZEN

THE RISE AND FALL OF LONDON'S MOST FEARED ARMED ROBBERY GANG

NOEL 'RAZOR' SMITH

JOHN BLAKE

Published by John Blake Publishing,
80–1 Wimpole Street,
Marylebone
London W1G 9RE

www.facebook.com/johnblakebooks
twitter.com/jblakebooks

First published in paperback in 2020

Paperback ISBN: 978-1-78946-226-5
Ebook ISBN: 978-1-78946-227-2
Audio ISBN: 978-1-78946-228-9

British Library Cataloguing-in-Publication Data:
A catalogue record for this book is available from the British Library.

Design by www.envydesign.co.uk

Printed and bound in Great Britain by Clays Ltd, Elcograf S.p.A.

1 3 5 7 9 10 8 6 4 2

John Blake Publishing is an imprint of Bonnier Books UK
www.bonnierbooks.co.uk

THE DIRTY
DOZEN

For my lovely wife,
Caroline Bateman Smith.
And for my agent, Cat Ledger.
May you rest in peace.

CONTENTS

'Every single time it was grand. I loved the moment when you announce the stickup, and everything suddenly goes brighter and sharper and the world seems to spin faster. You show them the gun and say "hand it over" and there's no telling what's going to happen in the next tick of the clock.'

James Carlos Blake, *Handsome Harry*

FOREWORD

The story you are about to read is all true. The Dirty Dozen were a real and serious armed-robbery gang from north-west London, who committed hundreds of raids on banks, security vans, Post Offices and travel agents. They stole hundreds of thousands of pounds during a decade-long crime spree. The leading lights of the gang were all second-generation Irish, the sons of Irish immigrants who had settled in London in the 1950s.

The original leader of the Dirty Dozen was 'Gentleman' Jimmy Doyle, a ruthless robber but with a touch of panache and style about him. Doyle had a good reputation in the criminal underworld as a staunch man. He was an old-fashioned bank robber who saw what he did as his job and took pride in his work. The gang never offered gratuitous violence to members of the public, though they were obviously expert at using the tools of violence, including threats, intimidation and aggression, in order to achieve their aims. Jimmy Doyle was eventually captured by the Flying Squad in the commission of a bank robbery in 1992 and, while on remand, he escaped custody and fled to Ireland. Extradited a year later, he was eventually sentenced to prison for twenty-four years at the Old Bailey in 1995. Two years later, he escaped from a prison van while being transported between prisons and disappeared off the radar for many years. Doyle died peacefully in Killorglin, Ireland, on 30 April 2013.

The unique thing about the Dirty Dozen was their fluidity and power of regeneration. Like the Hydra, you could cut off one of their heads and two more would immediately take its place. The original gang, led by Jimmy Doyle, fostered criminal understudies – younger gang members who were eager to step up when their time came – carrying on the traditions of those who had gone before. They had easy access to firearms, and the will and recklessness to get into the game and keep it running for as long as they were able.

Though the Dirty Dozen were a loose federation of criminals, their loyalty to each other was what helped them to reign for so long as kings of their trade. It must be borne in mind that in London there are special police squads dedicated to catching armed robbers, and only armed robbers – specifically, the Flying Squad, who make it their business to target armed-robbery gangs and to put not inconsiderable manpower and resources to work on the problem. The fact that the Dirty Dozen were active for so long proves that they were a tight-knit organisation.

Most members had grown up with each other and were very familiar with the rules, the unwritten criminal code that 'old skool' criminals attempt to live their criminal lives by. The number one rule is: no grassing.

When Jimmy Doyle and several other gang members were arrested, convicted and then jailed back in the 1990s, two contenders for the throne stepped forward. The Bradish brothers proved more than capable of assuming the mantle of vacant leadership. Under the Bradish boys, the Dirty Dozen flourished and added plenty to their gangland legends.

I first came across Sean and Vinnie Bradish when we were all serving long prison sentences as Category A prisoners in HMP Whitemoor, in Cambridgeshire (one of the highest-security prisons in Europe). I was serving eight life sentences under the two-strikes act for armed robbery and possession of firearms, having been sentenced at the Old Bailey in 1998 for a series of bank robberies. My gang were nicknamed 'The Laughing Bank Robbers' by the Flying Squad and the media. Sean and Vinnie were the last of the Dirty Dozen, and had been jailed in a blaze of publicity in 2000 on the testimony of a supergrass called Stephen Roberts.

In the media reports on the Bradish brothers' case, they were often compared to Grant and Phil Mitchell, the bad-boy brothers from BBC's long-running soap-opera *EastEnders*. This was mainly to do with the fact that the Bradish boys bore a passing resemblance to the actors who played the fictional Mitchells – they were both bald, Londoners and had a penchant for violence. But while the soap-opera Mitchells acted as hard men with fake guns, the Bradish boys were the real thing.

During their trial at the Old Bailey, Sean and Vinnie Bradish were named by the prosecution as 'the most prolific armed robbers this country has ever known'. They even appear in the *Guinness Book of Records* listed as such. Being charged with over fifty armed robberies each, one might assume that they must be incompetent or careless operators but, despite the police having them under intermittent surveillance for years without even a sniff of evidence, their downfall came through a betrayal by one of the close members of their gang.

Stephen Roberts, one of the Dirty Dozen who turned supergrass on his former friends and associates, now lives under an assumed name in the UK's version of the witness protection programme. In the course of this story, I came across many incidences of callous violence by Stephen Roberts during his time as a principle member of the gang and, just as in the case of the most infamous and first British supergrass, Bertie Smalls, many people believed that Roberts escaped justice when he was just as bad, if not worse, than the men he accused.

In order to write this book, I needed access to the people involved and where better to get the story than from the mouths of those involved. I am lucky enough to have access to some of those people, which allows me to present to you the true story of London's Dirty Dozen, Britain's most prolific armed-robbery gang.

NOEL 'RAZOR' SMITH

THE BEGINNING
OF THE END

'I would nick anything that wasn't nailed down.'
Stephen John Roberts (b.1966), supergrass

12 October 1999 – Paddington, London

The early evening is cold, even for October. It has been raining on and off all day and the streets around Paddington are drying in patches. A small blue Nissan car pulls out of traffic and parks on a single yellow line outside a mini-market shop. A tall white man in his thirties named Steve Wall exits the Nissan and walks casually into the shop while talking on his mobile phone. Inside the Nissan, a young female, Wall's girlfriend, sits in the front passenger seat, staring blankly through the windscreen, fiddling idly with a strand of her hair.

In the back-passenger seat, there is another white male in his thirties. Stephen Roberts is a dyed-in-the-wool criminal with a long police record for mugging, violence, possession of weapons and car theft. He is an impulsive and opportunistic thief, reckless and venal. He seems very switched-on compared to the female. His eyes are feral in the fading light, glancing this way and that, alert to the movements and directions of the few pedestrians on the pavement and the flow of traffic on the road. He watches the indicator flash of a dark green Rover 620, which pulls out of traffic and pulls in front of the Nissan. Stephen Roberts leans forward from the backseat of the Nissan, elbows on the top of the driver's seat, and watches the Rover intently.

The driver's door of the Rover swings open and a smart but casually dressed young black man steps out. He is also carrying a mobile phone. He looks around and glances at the Nissan and its two occupants for a moment, before heading across the short expanse of pavement. Stephen Roberts notices that the black man is not carrying his car keys and the lights of the Range Rover are still on. A slow smile touches his thin lips. He watches as the black man walks into the mini-market and, as soon as he disappears inside, Roberts taps the female passenger on the shoulder. 'Later,' he says, and slips out of the Nissan.

Roberts walks brazenly to the driver's door of the Range Rover and opens it. He looks at the ignition and his smile broadens as he sees the keys dangling there. In a couple of seconds, he is into the Rover, the engine starts, and he pulls out into the traffic without indicating. In under five minutes, the green Rover is parked up in the car park of a council estate less than a mile from where it was stolen, and Roberts is off on foot into the gathering gloom of the evening in NW10.

Meanwhile, back at the mini-market, the black man has realised his car is missing. He then notices that the male passenger who was in the Nissan is also nowhere to be seen. As Steven Wall exits the shop, the black man confronts him. An argument ensues, with Wall denying any knowledge or involvement in the theft of the motor. Steven Wall has known Stephen Roberts since they were children together on the notorious Stonebridge estate and has little doubt that Roberts has taken the man's car. It wasn't planned, just a spur-of-the-moment, opportunistic theft by a man who has been carrying out such acts throughout his life.

The argument becomes heated and, when Wall tries to push past the black man to get into his car, the man grabs a handful of Wall's T-shirt. Wall throws a punch at him and it all kicks off. The fight is short and bloody, with Wall getting the worst of it as several powerful blows are landed on his face and head. Inside the Nissan, his girlfriend is screaming at the man to stop. Eventually, Wall catches his opponent with a punch to the neck, which knocks him off balance and allows Wall the precious seconds he needs to get into his car and pull away.

Inside the Nissan, Steven Wall is cursing Stephen Roberts for leaving him wearing the paper hat, again. There is blood dripping from his nose and trickling from a cut above his right eyebrow and, as he drives, his girlfriend searches the glove compartment for a tissue. Wall drives fast and soon puts plenty of distance between himself and his still-fuming assailant. As he sits waiting for the traffic lights to change, his girlfriend dabs at the cut above his eyebrow with a dirty Kleenex. Wall punches the steering wheel hard. 'Roberts is a fucking cunt,' he says, angrily. 'A fucking liability. He needs fucking shooting, the slag.' His girlfriend clucks sympathetically as she continues cleaning the blood from his face. But she knows that Wall and Roberts are criminal partners and good friends, and that Wall's anger will soon dissipate.

Later that night, Stephen Roberts makes a call on his mobile. 'All right, mate? Got a motor for tomorrow.' The man on the other end of the phone is Sean Bradish. Sean is wise enough to assume that the police have probably got him under surveillance and are listening in on his phone calls. He is not 100 per cent sure, but always errs on the side of caution. 'OK,' Sean replies. 'Baked potato.' Then he cuts off the call.

Stephen Roberts is excited and not a little fearful. Stealing this car has just given him an in with the leader of one of London's most daring armed-robbery gangs. They were stealing the kind of cash he could only dream about, and he had long harboured a desire to join the gang. When the gang had been led by Jimmy Doyle, the likes of Roberts stood little chance of getting an invite to the big table. But now that Doyle had legged it for pastures new and the remnants of the old gang were banged up behind the high walls and razor-wire-festooned fences of HMP, Roberts had managed to make himself useful enough to get a shot. He was hoping to be invited on the Bradish boys next robbery.

13 October 1999 – Rosehill, Sutton

A late-model green Rover 620 turns off the Rosehill roundabout at Sutton, in the suburbs of south London at 10.15am. Rain is coming down heavily and the windscreen wipers are working overtime to clear sheets of water from the screen. Visibility is low, and tyres throw up hefty spray from the road as it turns into the large car park behind the Co-op supermarket. The car park is full of cars, but mostly devoid of people. The sparse foot traffic consists of people with their heads down against the rain or concealed in the shelter of umbrellas, and nobody even glances at the car as it comes to a stop in a bay towards the back of the car park.

Inside the car, the heater is on full blast and the radio is on low. Stephen Roberts sits in the driver's seat, tapping his fingers on the steering wheel. Roberts, in his early thirties, of medium height and build, with dark hair and slightly vulpine features, is wearing a black hooded sports top, jeans, Reebok Classic trainers and cream-coloured surgical gloves. Next to him sits Sean Bradish, six-foot of hard muscle, fair hair cropped to the bone and with a serious look of concentration in his steel-blue eyes. Bradish is wearing a green, ex-military hooded parka, jeans, black Nike trainers and cream-coloured surgical gloves. The only sounds are the low murmur of the morning deejay, the swoosh of the wipers, rush of the heater and tapping of the rain on the roof. Both men are staring intently through the windscreen.

After a short wait, a large, white Securitas cash-in-transit van pulls into the car park and stops close to the back door of the supermarket. Bradish reaches into the back seat and pulls a blue sports bag into the front passenger foot-well. He quickly unzips the bag and takes out a .22 semi-automatic pistol and a black bandanna, which he hands to Stephen Roberts, who tie ties it around the lower half of his face. Bradish takes an identical bandanna from the bag and covers his own face, flipping up the hood of his parka so that only his eyes and a thin strip of forehead is visible. He then pulls a Remington 16-gauge, single-barrelled shotgun from the bag. The gun is less than eighteen inches long, sawn off at both barrel and butt, and decorated with carvings of pheasants and other birds on its nickel-plated barrel. Bradish snaps the gun open and checks the red Ely birdshot cartridge. The shiny brass firing plate of the ammunition seems to glow in the gloomy interior of the car. Bradish snaps the shotgun shut, takes six spare cartridges from the bag and drops them into the large front pocket of his parka.

They watch as the uniformed security guard steps out of his van and straight into a puddle. He shakes water from his boots and walks to the small cash-chute door on the side of the van, where he stands for a couple of seconds, raindrops rolling down the Perspex visor of his helmet. After a quick glance around, which reveals nothing suspicious (visibility obviously being not great in the rain), the guard bangs his hand on the side of the van. The cash-chute door opens and an oblong security box is pushed down it by the custodian inside the back of the van. The box is about eighteen inches tall, grey in colour and with the Securitas logo on each side. The guard picks it up by the plastic handle and carries it into the supermarket.

Experienced robbers like Sean Bradish and Stephen Roberts know the steps of this dance intimately. Known in criminal parlance as a 'Pony' box[1], the security box is insured and able to hold up to £25,000 in cash. Logic told the waiting robbers that the first one going into the supermarket will be empty. The only people who take cash into a supermarket are customers; security firms take money out in order to bank it, so there is no point robbing the guard on his way in as you will only get an empty – or 'dummy' – box. The trick is to get the guard on the way back to the van with the cash.

Bradish takes a deep breath and steps out into the lashing rain. He closes the door of the car and holds the shotgun down, barrel facing the ground and close to his leg, out of sight of the casual observer. Roberts slips out of the driver's side, closes the door and puts his hood up. He keeps the .22 pistol in his pocket with his hand around it, finger on the trigger. The two men cross the wet and windy car park quickly and without fuss. They weave their way between the parked cars, eyes firmly fixed on the Securitas van and the back door to the supermarket close by, until they are about ten feet away from their

1 'Pony' is criminal slang for the number 25, brought into usage by servicemen returning from India in the nineteenth century, as Indian rupee bank notes had pictures of animals on them. The 25-rupee note had a horse on it, so 25 became known as a 'pony'. The 500-rupee note had a monkey on it, so 500 became known as a 'monkey'. This code was widely used by racecourse bookies in the 1920s and 1930s, and slipped into criminal parlance around that time.

target. Suddenly, there is the guard coming through the door, head down watching for puddles as he makes his way to the cash chute on the side of the van.

Bradish moves very quickly, and within six steps he is level with the guard. He grabs him by the collar of his uniform and swings him bodily into the side of the van. The guard is taken completely by surprise and lets out a yelp as he bounces off the van, still firmly in Bradish's grip. Then the barrel of the shotgun is under his nose, and he's looking at a gaping chasm that the guard knows, on a visceral level, is ready to spit death in a hot second. He looks into the merciless eyes of his assailant and knows, beyond any doubt, that this man will shoot him in the face if he does not comply. He is terrified.

The guard feels the box ripped from his fingers and sees the other masked and hooded man from the corner of his eye. He dares not look directly, as Bradish has him pinned to the van by a hand around his throat and the gun inches from his face. Roberts lifts the cash box above his head and flings it at the ground as hard as he can. There is a loud clunk as it hits the wet concrete, and a corner crumples. Roberts picks the box up quickly and launches it at the ground again with all the force he can muster. The box pops open and Roberts grabs the grey cloth cash bag contained within. He rifles through it and finds only receipts and cheques, which he scatters on the ground.

'No cash!' Roberts shouts. He takes the semi-automatic pistol from his pocket and pushes it hard into the guard's temple, knocking his head sideways.

'Where's the fucking money, you prick?' he screams into the guard's face.

Bradish is calm. He leans close to the guard's ear and tells him firmly, 'Call your mate in the back and tell him, if he doesn't put the cash out, we are going to shoot you.' The guard bobs his head up and down. By now he has both hands up and is held at the point of two guns, pressed against the side of his vehicle. He opens his mouth to shout but what comes out is a terrified croak. He clears his throat and shouts to the van custodian, 'Roy, they mean business, mate. They're not playing. Throw the money out, mate, please.' His voice cracks on the word 'please'.

For what seems like an eternity to all involved but, in actual fact, was probably around five seconds, nothing happens. The rain continues to fall heavily, and the metallic ping of raindrops richocheting off the vehicles seems very loud. Then a middle-aged woman exits the back door of the supermarket and stops dead when confronted with the tableaux in front of her. She screams loudly, drops her two heavy shopping bags and runs back into the building. Bradish is just about to let go of the guard and chalk this up to experience, when the cash chute opens and a grey cash box falls out. It hits the ground with a heavy thump and is followed by an identical box, which lands on top of it.

Roberts is on the cash boxes like shit off a hot shovel. He rips the lid from the first and finds a cash bag. Inside that are clear plastic packets of bank notes: tens and twenties. He snatches the lid from the second box and finds many more packets of money. He puts the pistol back into his pocket and gathers the cash bags. 'Got it!' he shouts, then turns and hurries back to the Rover. Sean lets go of the guard's neck and steps back. The guard's legs give way and he crumples to the wet ground and stays there, head down, not daring to look up, emotionally and mentally drained, paralysed with fear. By now a small crowd, alerted by the woman shopper, are gathering outside the back doors of the supermarket, watching. Several of them are talking urgently into their mobile phones. Bradish swings the shotgun towards them and they scuttle in all directions, like cockroaches exposed to sudden light. He lopes across the car park to his car.

The Rover speeds across the car park and out onto the roundabout. Roberts is driving as Bradish stuffs the guns, money, gloves and bandannas into the sports bag. He strips off his heavy parka and stuffs that into the bag too. Under the parka, he is wearing a bright-blue hoodie. As Roberts takes the first left off the roundabout, the sound of sirens can be heard coming from the direction in which they are heading. Half a mile from the scene of the robbery, as they drive by St Helier Hospital, two marked police cars, sirens wailing and lights flashing, head towards them. As the cars approach, Bradish reaches into the bag at his feet and grips the shotgun. If this is it, he won't go easy. But the police cars speed on down the road, unaware that they have just passed the men they are looking for.

A little further up the road, Bradish directs Roberts to turn left and park up. They are in a quiet residential street and Roberts pulls into a parking space and cuts the engine. In the relative quiet, they can hear many police sirens in the distance. Bradish grabs the bag and walks quickly further on up the road, followed by Roberts, who has taken off his hooded jacket and dropped it into a wheelie-bin as they pass. Bradish pulls a set of keys from his pocket and clicks the key fob. It emits a beep and the rear lights of a black F-reg BMW 360i flash. They climb into the car and this time, Bradish is driving. He takes it easy to avoid attracting police attention and heads for Sutton shopping centre two miles away.

After parking the BMW in the underground car park of the Holiday Inn, both men head inside to book a room. They give false names at the reception desk and take a double room for one night. They pay in cash. Once in the hotel room, with the door firmly locked, Bradish empties the sports bag onto the bed, and the count-up and share-out begins. The proceeds from the robbery add up to a total of £26,730 in cash. Over £13,000 each. Not bad for a day's work. At this point in time, Sean Bradish, Stephen Roberts and the rest of their gang had committed dozens of armed robberies and other crimes, and some of them were starting to think that they were untouchable. But, although they yet had no inkling of it, the days of London's most prolific armed-robbery crew – The Dirty Dozen – were coming to an end.

CHAPTER ONE

DIRTY DOZEN ORIGINS

There have always been geographical anomalies when it comes to crime in England, and none more so than in the capital. In Gilbert Kelland's book *Crime in London* (1986), he claims that, in the mid-1980s, about eighty-five per cent of all serious armed robberies committed in the whole of England were carried out by a small pool of men from south London. Since the early 1960s, north-west London, along with Bermondsey in south London, has earned a reputation for producing ruthless and violent armed-robbery gangs. They are usually working-class young men, who have grown up in the poverty of those two areas and feel that, due to class, position and lack of opportunities for advancement, they have little choice but to choose crime. Or it could just be that they are greedy, lazy, work-shy bandits with no respect for the rule of law and with a brazen arrogance. Or maybe it's something in the water – who knows?

The Stonebridge estate in Brent, north-west London, was named after the stone bridge, built in 1745, that allowed Harrow Road to cross the River Brent. Until the late nineteenth century, this was the site of Stonebridge Farm and Willesden's first sewage works. During the 1950s, the council planned a massive redevelopment covering almost a hundred acres. More than two thousand units were built, mostly in high-rise blocks, the first of which opened in 1967. Despite the council's good intentions, the Stonebridge estate soon proved flawed in design and execution, and residents felt that little interest was shown in their welfare. The body of an elderly tenant, John Sheppard, was discovered in 1993 after he had lain dead in his flat for three years. It is fair to say that this estate had a reputation for crime, drug dealing and violence almost since its inception.

For the local criminals, the Stonebridge was a magnet. Empty flats could be squatted and turned into crack houses or storage for weapons and stolen goods. The estate was a maze and easy for criminals to escape the police. A lot of the Dirty Dozen gang either grew up on the estate or gravitated towards it when they were teenagers. A pub on the outskirts of the estate – The Coach & Horses – became a meeting place for the local villains. It was in this pub on a fateful evening in 1995 that Sean and Vinnie Bradish, already leading members of the gang, first met the man who was eventually to be responsible for their downfall: Stephen Roberts.

Committing armed robbery is not a career for the faint-hearted. It takes a lot of bottle to go and put yourself on offer when you know that the end result could be bundles of years in prison (rarely does a professional armed robber get less than double figures when it comes to sentencing), or even death. It is common for armed police to shoot dead those men who are in the commission of armed robbery. British police do not shoot to wound, they shoot to 'stop' or, in plain language, to kill. The list of criminals shot dead by the police in this country is pretty long and, as a bonus for the police, not one of the police shooters has ever been convicted of a crime for these judicial killings. So choosing to enter an enterprise that could very easily result in your own death is a bit of a reckless move.

A lot of the men – for it is a predominantly male occupation – who become armed robbers do not drift into it, like you would with some smaller-scale crimes; they actively choose it. Despite the dangers of a career like armed robbery, the rewards can be massive in monetary terms. When infamous American bank robber Willie Sutton (1901-80) was asked by a newspaper reporter why he chose to rob banks, he replied, 'Because that's where the money is.' And it really is as simple as that for some people.

Armed robbers, on the whole, are get-rich-quick gamblers, willing to risk it all on the chance that they will hit the big one. The prize for them is stealing large amounts of ready cash with the minimum of effort. The average bank robbery takes around four minutes from start to finish. Though, for the people involved, especially the victims, it can seem as though it's a lot longer.

The Bradish gang were great at robbing on spec, which means just going out onto the streets and looking for a target. If you are at it, you have to be aware that there are always going to be wrong'uns who will be earwigging your plans, or people who see you with a bit of cash and a new car who will get envious and decide to report their suspicions about you to the authorities. So going out on spec has its advantages. For a start, the police will not be able to set up a ready-eye ambush because they do not know where you are going to strike. A lot of robbers are either arrested or shot dead after being ambushed by the Flying Squad, usually because they have been under surveillance after a tip-off. The smart money says that the less people who know what you are doing, the better.

Going out on spec is also a bit like a Forest Gump's box of chocolates when it comes to the prize: you just never know what you're going to get. The average bank robbery will pay less than £10,000 if you are robbing till-money – i.e. not leaping the counter or trying to get at the vault where the bulk of the readies are kept. Sometimes bank robbers get very lucky and manage to make their escape with a nice chunk of change if they happen to hit at the moment when there is a cash delivery, or a large amount being paid in by a customer. But ten grand for four minutes' work is still a pretty good rate of pay.

On the whole, most bank robberies are carried out by chancers who need quick cash. The professional bank robber can only make a living from robbing banks because they know what they are doing. They will time their robbery for when the delivery is being made, or for when they know the tills are heavy with notes. The way they get information on this sort of thing is through what the police and prison authorities would call 'intelligence' – basically, a lot of experience, trial and error and, of course, through talking to people. Criminals – and, in particular, robbers – are normally quite personable people who love talking to members of the public, particularly ones who work anywhere that money or valuables are being held. There is plenty of useful information out there for criminals. They just have to know how to harvest it.

So the essential ingredients needed to commit armed robbery are plenty of bottle, ruthlessness, the ability to act aggressively and make people believe that you would rather kill them than get the money, a certain amount of intelligence, and recklessness. You will also need a weapon, a disguise and a getaway car. If you have all of those things, you could go to work right now. The Bradish boys had all of these things and, boy, did they go to work.

CHAPTER TWO

THE 'AYATOLLAH' AND THE GENESIS OF THE DIRTY DOZEN

The original Dirty Dozen gang was set up and led by a second-generation Irishman called James 'Jimmy' Doyle. Doyle became the leader of the Dirty Dozen in the early 1980s, when times were hard and money was short and a lot of young tearaways with no real direction in life and very few prospects began to realise that, if they wanted 'the life' that Margaret Thatcher's 'Greed is Good' acolytes were touting, they had better get out there and take it.

Doyle was born in Ballinskelligs, County Kerry, in 1965. His parents, along with little Jimmy, emigrated to England soon after he was born. Settling in the Wembley district of north-west London, the family were not rich by any means, and Jimmy wore his share of hand-me-down clothes. Being immigrants, poor and speaking with a country Irish accent, little Jimmy had to toughen up. He had a lot of fights trying to fit in to his new London home. Like most poor kids, Jimmy dreamed of a day when he would be able to afford the luxuries of life, like cars, brand-new clothes and jewellery. He loved watching crime films, especially heist movies, and it was probably this interest that got him thinking that this might be the life for him.

Jimmy Doyle was what is known in criminal parlance as a 'money-getter'. These are criminals for whom crime seems to come easy and who have more than their fair share of luck when taking the prize. Jimmy was never greatly academic, but he had a natural cunning and a ruthless streak when it came to crime. He started off making money in the usual way of street kids everywhere: bringing empty bottles back to shops and off-license premises for deposits. He received three old pennies for every bottle he brought in, so Jimmy got to thinking that there must be a better way to boost that bit of pocket money. He worked out that, if he went around the back of the shop and climbed over a wall, he would be in the yard where the bottles were stored and be able to help himself to however many bottles he wanted. But the first time he climbed the wall, he noticed that he ripped the knee out of his jeans. In typical Jimmy Doyle fashion, he decided that it would be easier if he got someone else to do the climbing.

He put together his first little gang with a couple of boys he knew from school and, for the next couple of months, they had a relatively lucrative business. The plan was simple: Jimmy would grab a couple of empty wooden fruit boxes and place them up against the off-license's back wall and then get his two companions to climb the wall. One would sit on top of the wall and the other would go into the yard and hand the precious bottles up. Jimmy would take the bottles from the lad on the wall and bag them. When they had a nice few bottles, they would go and cash them in. Some businesses would stamp the label of their bottles with their logo and would only take returns with that same logo, but other shops did not give a toss and would happily pay out for anyone's bottles.

The idea of getting others to take the risks while he raked in the rewards was something that never really left Jimmy and was to become one of his favourite moves. At the age of twelve, he was already thinking like a major gang boss. The division of labour with himself at the top, out of harm's way, seemed to be Jimmy's future plan. The value of this strategy was brought home to him when the gang were rumbled by the owner of the off-license they were stealing the bottles from. As they were in mid-steal, the owner came into his backyard and caught them red-handed. That is, he caught two of them: the kid in the yard and the kid on the wall. When Jimmy heard the shout, he was on his toes before the second syllable of the owner's words hit the air. Jimmy legged it back to his house and went about his business with an air of unsullied innocence.

In the event, he learned another valuable lesson from this incident. When the two boys were grabbed by the scruff of their necks and dragged into the off-license to face the music, they both crumbled like dried-up poundcake and couldn't wait to name Jimmy as a confederate. Eventually, a local police officer turned up at the Doyle household to have a word with young Jimmy. With the brass-neck of an American preacher begging for a new 'Jesus jet', Jimmy denied that he had ever even seen a lemonade bottle in his life, let alone formed a gang to heist them. Sticking up his choirboy face and looking the bobby straight in the eye, he seemed to be saying, 'Nick me, copper, or get off the pot.' As it was really a petty theft, no further action was taken. But Jimmy had a lot to think about if he wanted to make crime his living. He now knew that he would look carefully at the habits and characters of anyone he would choose to commit any skullduggery with in the future. 'Trust no one, except yourself' was to become Jimmy's mantra for life.

Jimmy Doyle labored under a couple of nicknames that were complete opposites in the criminal world. This showed the two sides of his personality. He made it a personal point to always be polite in his dealings with everyone. 'It's nice to be nice' was one of the sayings that Jimmy loved, but the other side of the coin was 'fuck with me and I'll kill you.' A complicated man, loved by some and hated by others, Jimmy's most persistent nickname was 'Gentlemen' Jimmy, and that was because, for most of the time, he could be a charming and personable fellow. Though Doyle could be very ruthless with his gang, in everyday life he was a soft-spoken, genial and polite man; he respected women and always had a smile and a kind word for whomever he met. People liked Jimmy: he had charm.

Then there was Jimmy's criminal persona, known in the underworld as the 'Ayatollah' due to his ruthless leadership style. It is said that after a pretty lucrative robbery he noticed that a member of the gang had taken more than his fair share of the takings. Jimmy flew into an immediate rage and beat the gang-member unconscious with the first item that came to hand, which in this case was a frozen chicken. He ruthlessly bounced the frozen fowl off his confederate's face, breaking his nose. When it came to money, nobody had better take a liberty when the Ayatollah was in charge.

It was in the local villain's watering-hole of the Coach & Horses on the Stonebridge that Jimmy usually held court. And this was where the Bradish brothers first got a hunger to follow in Jimmy's footsteps. Vinnie's recollection of these shady characters reads like a scene from Martin Scorsese's mob classic *Goodfellas*.

Every other week they'd be in the pub with bundles of money. It was never ending. They were doing it all the time. Nice suits on them and it seemed like the police couldn't catch anyone and so I said to myself, in the end, this is ridiculous, and I got involved with it myself. They've been doing it for so long, they've obviously got it mastered so I looked into it. Me and Sean started up and that was it. I did my own planning and I liked it even more. Planning from A to B, doing the surveillance, hiding here, ducking there, looking at different escape routes, how to get out of places, what if this happened, what if that happened, plan A, plan B, if this goes wrong, go that way, if that goes wrong... Checking it all out, making sure that the job goes properly. I liked all that. It was good then and you could do what you wanted. It was a good buzz. I liked it because it was like a game – who's out-smarting who.

In later years, when he had made his fortune through armed crime, Jimmy Doyle was always surrounded by beautiful women. He loved to wear Armani, Hugo Boss and Gucci suits while snorting cocaine and downing pink champagne at swanky wine bars and London nightclubs. His childhood dreams were coming true. Exotic holidays with his girlfriends and fellow gang members were other favourites of the charismatic criminal known to everyone as 'Gentleman Jimmy'. It was through Jimmy Doyle that the Bradish boys learned the true art of crossing the pavement. And Doyle was the master at it. He was a smart and cunning career criminal.

He soon realised that, if he only ever attacked small targets where the takings were never too high and switched tactics while using different members of the his loosely confederated gang, the Dirty Dozen, to carry out the robberies, the Old Bill would think the raids were the work of random amateurs instead of one single gang. Jimmy started targeting bookmakers' offices and, when the Flying Squad suspected the raids might be linked, he immediately moved on to building societies and then the banks. The gang's largest ever take was only £36,000 but, with Doyle carrying out sometimes two heists a week, there was always more than enough money to go round – and this is how it would go down.

Two gang members would steal two cars for the getaway on the morning of the raid. Jimmy would choose the target but very rarely go inside himself, opting instead to supervise the heist from a nearby phone box or other vantage point. The robbery itself would be carried out by two gunmen with a driver waiting outside. Access to weaponry was never a problem for the Dirty Dozen, with Doyle stashing sixteen guns and thousands of rounds of ammunition in bank safety deposit boxes. Wearing masks or crash helmets, the two men would burst in. One would empty the tills while the other kept guard and a close eye on the time to ensure the robbery was done and dusted before the automatic alarm system kicked in.

During Doyle's trial at the Old Bailey, Judge Nina Lowery described him as a 'very dangerous criminal.' His raids, it was revealed, were 'executed with something akin to military efficiency. His tactics of surprise and speed were nearly always successful. It was very difficult for the police to discover who was responsible. 'There are a number of features in this case which make it exceptionally grave,' she went on. 'The robberies were ruthless, and people were put into dreadful fear.'

Prosecutor Jonathan Laidlaw said Doyle 'was the senior member' and organised the team of six or seven as 'a tight and close-knit unit'.

The court heard how the gang holidayed together and some gang members had romantic connections with the female relatives of others. The guns used were kept in two secure stores one a safety deposit box on the Finchley Road, Hampstead, the other a lock-up on the

Abbey Industrial Estate, Wembley. Records kept by the security companies indicated the stores were visited just before a robbery was due to take place and again just after. Each raid was run on the original template that Jimmy had perfected through experience: gang members would burst into the bank, don balaclavas and snatch the cash after pointing guns at terrified customers and staff. Most of the robberies took no more than four minutes to complete and, in some cases, one of the crew urged his accomplices on by shouting out how long they had been in the bank. Firearms were always loaded and, on one occasion, a shot was fired inside the bank. After another raid, a police motorcyclist was fired on during the gang's escape and was fortunate to escape injury.

Doyle's gang had no jitters about shooting at the police; they took the robbery game very seriously indeed, and they knew that armed police would have no worries about shooting at them. It was this tit-for-tat attitude of both robbers and police that put the public in so much danger; both sides were more than willing to fire shots in public in order to achieve their aims. In the case of the robbers, their prime aim was to escape with or without the prize, although preferably with. Jimmy Doyle viewed it like this: the fox is chasing for his dinner but the rabbit is running for his life. Therefore, the rabbit is entitled to fire a few back at his predator. Nobody wanted to actually kill anyone – that would lead to life sentences – but nobody wanted to spend years in prison either. Shooting or perhaps killing a police officer would bring a terrible heat down on the gang so, after a police motorcyclist was fired at, Jimmy Doyle had a serious chat with his boys about being a bit careful letting the shots off. His advice was, 'Fire as a last resort, and only if your liberty is on the line. And try not to kill anyone, especially Old Bill.'

For months, the Flying Squad had nothing to go on. The Doyle gang just seemed to pop up on an irregular basis, commit their robberies and then disappear back into the mean streets of London. The Flying Squad could see the evidence in front of their eyes. Robberies were happening on their patch but the perpetrators, though using the same method of operation (MO), appeared to be physically different and the targets were many and varied.

It was only when members of the squad looked closely at the security tapes from a robbery on the Alliance and Leicester building society in Station road, Harrow, that they noticed something. The gang had raided the Royal Bank of Scotland in nearby Harrow Road in February 1992, and then again the following September. The building society camera had been focused on the street outside and both tapes showed Doyle and an accomplice after the robbery. Doyle was known to the police and this gave them something to work on. They immediately set up a surveillance operation on Jimmy Doyle and his accomplice and, from there, they eventually managed to identify several members of the robbery gang.

Doyle's gang had thought they were great at anti-surveillance; they were very careful about who they talked to and did not really trust anyone who was not in the gang. But this was instrumental in allowing the police to identify them once they had an identity for Doyle. Almost everyone the gang were meeting while under police surveillance were criminals; fellow robbers. Once the police had identified the nucleus of the gang, it was a waiting game. As I have mentioned before, the ideal situation for the Flying Squad would be to actually catch them straight after the commission of a robbery. The Flying Squad set up Operation Crozon in order to catch the gang red-handed. (If anyone is wondering how the police come up with such names for their operations, I can tell you that it is purely random. A police computer throws out the names as each operation is entered.)

The Dirty Dozen robberies carried out by Jimmy Doyle's gang had started in the summer of 1988 and carried on for the next four years. It was in March 1992 that Jimmy decided to take a back seat and let his gang do the heavy lifting. By this time, Jimmy was starting to think that he was now invincible. After all, he had committed over a hundred armed robberies without (as far as he was concerned) even a sniff from the Flying Squad and he was living the high life, with foreign holidays four or five times a year, designer clothes, top-of-the-range cars and plenty of beautiful women. What could possibly go wrong?

For months the Flying Squad watched every movement made by their prey. In everyday life, the gang were pretty careful to check their backs and keep an eye open for tails and spies, but their anti-surveillance really kicked in on the day before a job was to go off. The squad knew they had to really creep around with this gang and not take any chances. They set up Observation Posts (OPs) on the main players, including Doyle, so that they could record their comings and goings. They took long-range photos of each member of the gang and photographed all vehicles that the gang even had a passing acquaintance with. They knew the gang's routine as well as they knew their own. Now they had to catch them at it.

Doyle's gang was finally caught in an armed-police ambush in September 1992, after a £3,810 raid on Lloyds Bank in North Harrow, north-west London. It was the culmination of a £10 million Flying Squad operation that had involved up to 150 police officers, all of whom had studied Doyle's methods and targets. A tell-tale sign of a Doyle gang robbery was the choice of getaway cars – Vauxhall Astras. Four-door family cars that were big enough and nippy enough for the robbers getaway, and unobtrusive enough to blend in with other traffic.

At the time of his arrest, Jimmy was keeping watch for his crew of Kevin Jones and Jason Nicholas. In his back pocket were travel details for another holiday, this time in Trinidad. By sheer coincidence, a television camera crew were shadowing the Flying Squad for a TV series and managed to capture the unfolding drama on film.

Lloyds Bank in Harrow was one of the newer bank buildings. Straddling a junction between Pinner Road and Harrow Road, it featured an alleyway at the back of the premises between the bank and Harrow library that led to a fenced-in car park. There was a public phone box at the side of the bank from where the bank and approaching roads could be observed. On 9 September 1992, Jimmy Doyle's gang decided to rob this bank. Two days before the robbery, the gang took possession of a stolen red Vauxhall Astra. The car was seen being driven by one of the gang, who were already under surveillance. As the gang had previous for using stolen Vauxhall Astras on past robberies, the police decided to set up a watch on the car. Sure enough, on the morning of 9 September, there was a bit of suspicious activity around the car and the Flying Squad were hoping that it was going to be used. They watched as 'Target 4' Kevin Jones and 'Target 7' Jason Nicholas checked out the car and started it up. The men then left the car where it was and drove their own red Peugeot to pick up 'Target 1' Jimmy Doyle.

They had previously watched Jimmy Doyle and 'Target 2' Kevin O'Halloran doing a recce on two banks, and the Harrow branch of Lloyds seemed the likely target. The Flying Squad set up several OPs in order to keep watch on the possible targets and knew that now it was a waiting game.

The thing is, robbers like Doyle have a finely tuned sense of danger and suspicion and have no desire to hand a victory to the police and spend a huge chunk of their lives in prison so, to them, double-checking every detail of their surroundings is second nature. The Flying Squad had six armed officers plotted up in one of the houses across the road from the bank. They were watching the side of the bank, including the phone box and alley leading to the car park. In all, there were twenty-seven officers plotted up on the nearby streets in various unmarked vehicles. The specialist firearms officers – those with automatic shotguns and Heckler

& Koch sub-machine guns – were in two grey Range Rovers, known as 'gunships', which were just outside the immediate vicinity but ready to speed in when they got the word.

After a while, the figure of Jimmy Doyle could be seen walking up the street towards the bank. As he walked, seemingly casually to any unsuspecting bystander, his eyes were everywhere. He scanned the windows of every house on the street, watching for any movement or shadow that might be a tell-tale sign of a surveillance operation. The Flying Squad officers on the first floor of one of the premises opposite the bank had to crouch down and keep well away from the windows in case they were spotted.

Doyle walked around the area for a good twenty minutes, passing the bank several times before he seemed satisfied that the area was clear of police. He then ensconced himself in the public phone box and pretended to be on the phone while still scanning the street and surrounding area. After a short while, the stolen red Vauxhall Astra came along Pinner Road and parked up further down from the bank. Kevin Jones and Jason Nicholas, dressed casually in jeans and hooded sports tops, emerged from the Astra and began to walk slowly towards the bank. As they passed the phone box where Doyle was clearly visible, Jones nodded slightly to him.

Jones and Nicholas reached the front of the bank and walked straight past, eyes scanning everywhere. They then walked around the block before going back to the car. In the television footage of the incident, a Flying

Squad Sergeant in the OP across from the bank is heard to remark, 'They're so good! Especially for youngsters.'

When Jones and Nicholas emerged again from the car, they were seen to be tucking things into their pockets. This time, they walked towards the bank entrance with more purpose. As they reached the cashpoint machine by the door of the bank, they stopped for a moment and pulled ski-masks from their pockets and slipped them on. Jones pulled a Smith & Wesson revolver from his waistband and the two robbers entered the bank.

Outside, the police were hurriedly preparing to take their targets down. The police officers in the OP across from the bank put on their chequered police caps (so that they could be distinguished from the robbers when the action started), picked up their firearms and headed down the stairs to wait at the front door for the signal to attack. Meanwhile, over at the bank, an elderly man walked into the premises and, after seeing the robbery in progress, immediately ran back out. On seeing the man run out of the bank, somebody called over the radio, 'ATTACK! ATTACK! ATTACK!' – the police signal to move in.

Luckily for the police, it was only a couple of seconds after the elderly running man emerged that the robbers themselves make an appearance. Having stolen just over £4,000 in less than two minutes, Jones shouted to the cashiers on his way out, 'Thanks, girls. Have a nice day!'

The two robbers burst out of the bank at speed and ran around the side of the building towards where their getaway car was parked. The Flying Squad officers situated across the road from the bank were already on the street when the two robbers came bombing away from the crime scene, and they wasted no time in launching into a run themselves.

Suddenly, this previously quiet London street became a maelstrom of shouts from running police officers as they closed in on the robbers. Doyle, shocked at how quickly this was happening, replaced the handset in the phone box back on its cradle and turned on his heel to walk away and distance himself from what was going on. His two confederates ran straight past him. They were aware now that the police had been waiting for them, so it became not so much a getaway but more a foot race with the Flying Squad. Jason Nicholas was ahead of Kevin Jones. The baby-faced robber was as fit as a butcher's dog and he started to pull away from the many Flying Squad officers who were now in hot pursuit and closing.

Kevin Jones was grabbed by a Flying Squad Sergeant and brought to the ground. He was swiftly surrounded by armed officers, who were pointing pistols at his face and screaming for him not to move. Jason Nicholas got all the way down the alley and was in the process of vaulting a wooden fence into the car park when he was brought down by two large officers armed with handguns.

Doyle was snatched up as he turned to walk away, and he feigned innocence right from the start. His planned defence would be, 'Nothing to do with me, guv. I was just making a phone call.'

Once all three robbers had been plasti-cuffed and searched for weapons, the questioning began at the roadside. Jones was asked for his name but, when he replied, 'Kevin Jones,' the police did not believe him.

One Flying Squad officer said to him, 'Don't be silly. Stop giving obviously false names. Now what's your name?'

Despite his position, Jones showed irritation at this. 'My name is Kevin Jones,' he reiterates, more firmly.

On the film, you can see the shock and devastation on the faces of all three robbers, though Jimmy Doyle hides his behind a kind of *faux* outraged innocence. The Flying Squad are delighted at the result of a long, expensive and painstaking operation, and it shows on their faces. You can also detect the relief that no shots had been fired and nobody was hurt.

The robbery career of 'Gentleman' Jimmy Doyle was finally over, and the rise of the Dirty Dozen gang had been curtailed. For now. After spending three days being questioned at Wembley Police Station, the three robbers were remanded in custody to HMP Wormwood Scrubs to await trial.

But before Doyle could be brought to court, he escaped. The Doyle escape was only to be expected. Jimmy Doyle was not a man to turn spaniel and accept his fate; that was not part of his make-up. He was a fighter and, while there was even the slightest chance of getting away, he would keep fighting. Through his contacts outside – other members of the gang who had not yet been arrested – Jimmy Doyle made arrangements for an escape.

While in custody, Jimmy compained that he needed to see an eye specialist, because he was in pain. It seemed a reasonable request, as Doyle had always had trouble with his left eye, and had regularly attended Moorfield Eye Hospital as an outpatient since he was a kid. The prison arranged a visit to Moorfield Eye Hospital for Jimmy. While he was there, a masked man entered the building with a firearm and forced the prison escort staff to take Jimmy's cuffs off, and he made his escape.

Jimmy Doyle headed for the one place that he knew he would be safe: back home to Ireland.

He was eventually arrested there in August 1983 and extradited back to London. Extra-tight security surrounded the eight-week trial, with the jury of five men and seven woman receiving round-the-clock police protection, while armed police patrolled outside the locked courtroom. Jimmy's last job was also caught on film by a camera crew who were shooting a TV documentary, *Scotland Yard*, at the scene of the ambush. The footage was used in court to help convict Doyle of conspiracy to rob, which he denied. Doyle was charged with twenty-six robberies over a sixteen-month period leading up to his first arrest. However, police believed that Jimmy actually carried out 104 raids over a 4-year period – the longest string of robberies on their records in Britain – netting hundreds of thousands of pounds. O'Halloran, Jones and Nicholas had already been jailed for at least twenty years. Almost inevitably, the cocky Doyle laughed as the jury found him guilty, waved to friends and family in the public gallery, and was still grinning as he was led away to the cells by armed police.

Though the original nucleus of the Dirty Dozen was now

serving many years in prison, some of the younger members were still on the loose. The 'Ayatollah' had fallen, but the gang that he had created was already being replenished by younger members who now found themselves as up-and-comers. Soon-to-be supergrass Stephen Roberts – a Dublin-raised, Kilburn-based member of the gang – recalls:

I met Doyle a few times and he was an absolute lunatic. He spent as much time working on his wardrobe as he did planning the robberies. It all came on top for him when he was caught red-handed in 1995 and sent down to await trial. While he was on remand, he convinced the prison to let him go to Moorfields Hospital in London about this long-standing problem he had with his eye. He'd been a few times before and knew the place well. After his appointment, he asked to go to the toilet and, once he was inside, some bloke runs in with a shotgun, forces the coppers escorting him to get on the floor, then unlocks the handcuffs. He got away for a while but ended up getting caught in Ireland and sent down for twenty-four years at the Old Bailey. By a stroke of sheer luck, Sean and Vincent Bradish were having a day off when Doyle was picked up, so they were still out and about when the rest of the gang got put behind bars. They had a little break, then decided to carry on, forming their own little firm.

In April 2013, the body of Jimmy Doyle was discovered at his home in St James's Gardens, Killorglin, County Kerry.

Doyle had returned to his familial home upon his release the previous year, settling down a short distance from where his parents now lived in Ballinskelligs. Jimmy was only forty-eight years old at the time of his death and, although the Gardai ruled out foul play, his family and friends maintain he was the subject of constant harassment by the local Irish police. He was buried in the tranquil hills of South Kerry.

As for the rest of Doyle's original Dirty Dozen gang, like their one-time leader, they could not leave criminality alone – it was too lucrative. They served their prison sentences for armed robbery and, while in prison – our real universities of further criminal learning – they gained the knowledge and the contacts that would enable them to branch out in the criminal world.

In April 2016, Malcolm O'Halloran, a staunch lieutenant in the Doyle gang, and 'Target 2' to the Flying Squad, was jailed for sixteen years after cocaine worth up to £12 million was found in his van. Now aged fifty-one, O'Halloran was arrested after the drugs were discovered on the M1 in Hertfordshire on 19 January of the same year. The officers involved found 50 kg of cocaine stashed in a holdall. Three Russian handguns hidden in a coffee table were also found at his home, along with bundles of £20 notes behind a tumble dryer totaling £53,000.

He admitted six charges and was jailed for sixteen years at St Albans Crown Court. The judge said he was involved in a 'sophisticated' operation. Prosecutor Michael Speak said that other members of the drug network had been tracking O'Halloran through his phone. They must have launched a 'remote command' once they realised he had been arrested, which wiped any data connecting them to him, he said. The cocaine was mostly 83 per cent purity, with a street value of between £8.3 and £12.5 million. In total, £57,408 was found in various places around his rented home in Borehamwood.

O'Halloran admitted possession of cocaine with intent to supply, possession of criminal property, three charges of possessing guns and one of possessing ammunition. Clare Davies, defending, said he had been a courier who was paid £3,000 to transport the drugs, while he was storing the guns and cash for others. The court heard that O'Halloran had seventeen previous convictions, and Judge Stephen Warner said, as he passed sentence, that O'Halloran had been providing a 'safe house' for the guns and cash and had 'played a willing part' in the distribution network.

Detective Chief Inspector Chris Balmer said, 'Fifty kilograms of cocaine equates to an untold amount of misery and degradation on the streets of the eastern region, and the guns and cash found at his house demonstrate both the money involved with the drugs trade and the dangerous undercurrent of violence that comes with it.'

CHAPTER THREE

THE BRADISH BOYS: MAD AS A BOX OF FROGS

'The Bradish brothers are fucking mad. Know what I mean? It's like something in them just don't give a fuck. Them two are criminals twenty-four/seven.'
Stephen Roberts

August 1999 – Cricklewood, London

Most of the shops on Cricklewood Broadway were shut or shutting as evening crept its way over the brick-and-granite canyons of north-west London. The traffic was light – mainly low-powered mopeds with huge, square boxes attached to the back advertising the delivery services of myriad fast-food outlets. The twenty-four-hour mini-marts and chicken shops dotted along the street were like brightly lit islets in a sea of near-gloom. The electric street lights automatically switched on as the sun sank behind the high-rise flats and imparted a wan orange glow as they powered up. Foot traffic was sparse.

Outside the Allied Irish Bank, a white security van was parked. Two uniformed cash-in-transit guards emerged from the vehicle, both carrying large metal cash boxes.

The guards crossed the short expanse of pavement to the front door of the bank at a brisk pace. Both kept their heads up, eyes scanning their surroundings for anything out of the ordinary. They reached the entrance to the bank without incident, unlocked the outer door and slipped inside. Both guards breathed a small sigh of relief as they closed and locked the inner door of the bank and placed the boxes on the carpeted floor next to the cash machines. Being a cash-in-transit guard in London, or any of the big cities for that matter, was fraught with danger. Cash-in-transit robberies were on the increase and northwest London was a hot-spot. The guards began to unlock the boxes and stack the plastic-wrapped bundles of bank notes next to the four cash machines.

The mini-cab was a Ford Mondeo estate. The vehicle looked like it belonged in a breaker's yard; there was a large dent on the rear passenger-door and several smaller dents and scrapes evenly distributed around the body of the car. The wing-mirror had black masking tape wrapped around it to keep it in place, but it looked as though it was about to detach at any minute. The driver was a Rastafarian with deep-set yellow eyes and clumps of dusty-looking dreadlocks piled onto his head like a misshapen hat. He chewed a matchstick and looked straight ahead through the grimy, cracked windscreen.

'Twelve poun', init,' he said, his voice a deep bass.

Sean stepped out of the back of the car and slammed the door so hard the whole vehicle shook. He straightened his black tie and pulled at his suit to get a slight crease out of the material. It had been Sean's idea to dress up in the suits. He thought they looked classy, but he was now starting to regret it. The evening was too warm and the jacket was a bit too tight under the arms. Besides, he now thought, who the fuck wears a silk suit to the Galtymore Club? He looked over at his brother, Vinnie, who was emerging from the other side of the car, also suited and booted.

'Are you going to pay this eejit? Cos I'm fucking not.'

Vinnie smiled, but it was his 'don't fucking start' smile. Sean was younger than Vinnie by four years and, though they looked very similar – both were going bald in their early thirties so had shaved their heads, both had intense blue eyes – the two had completely different personalities. Lots of people thought that Sean was the older brother because he was bigger than Vinnie and was always the more serious. Sean, at 6 foot, was an inch taller and carried an air of menace about him. He was quick-tempered and quicker to offer violence to anyone who he thought was taking the piss. In Sean's eyes, almost everybody and anything was taking the piss.

Vinnie was the calmer of the brothers, much more easy-going and good-humoured. He preferred to treat people as he found them. It's nice to be nice, as his father used to say. That's not to say that Vinnie was any slowcoach when it came to putting the cosh about. He could be as violent as his brother if needs be, but violence was not his default setting like it was with Sean. Vinnie stepped up to the driver's door and looked through the open window at the driver for a moment.

'Listen,' he said. 'We're not tourists, brother. The fare from where you picked us up to here is six quid, max.' He reached into his pocket and pulled out a £10 note and held it between two fingers. 'There's the fare, plus a four-quid tip. Now you can take it... or...'

The driver slowly turned his head and eyed the £10 note for a second. He then looked out the far window at Sean standing with a scowl on his face, cracking his knuckles. The Rasta kissed his teeth loudly then snatched the money, threw the car into gear and screeched off into the gathering gloom.

Vinnie laughed out loud as he watched the single working tail-light disappear into the distance. The two brothers stood on the pavement under a streetlight. Sean pulled out a pack of cigarettes and lit one with a gold Ronson lighter. He blew a cloud of blue-grey smoke into the warm evening air.

'You're fucking mad giving that head-the-ball a tenner, Vin,' Sean said. 'I hate cunts who try ripping people off!'

Vinnie raised an eyebrow and gave his brother an incredulous look. 'Is that you talking, Sean? Are you serious? Do you even know who the fuck we are?'

Sean took another drag on his smoke but couldn't hide a little smile as he realised the absurdity of what he had said. 'Well...' he continued. 'You know what I mean.'

Vinnie shook his head. 'Sometimes I wonder about you, bruv.' He glanced at his watch: a wafer-thin gold

Bulova. 'Right, it's ten past nine. Where exactly are we meeting the girls?'

Sean took a final pull on his cigarette and then flicked it into the darkness of the middle of the road. He watched as several small glowing embers bounced on the warm tarmac. 'They're going to be waiting outside the Galtymore.' He looked down the road towards the Galtymore nightclub. He could see the lights in the distance.

Vinnie shook his head again. Another thing about Sean was his paranoia. Vinnie knew that his brother was more than 'careful' in everything he did. Being a professional criminal, he understood there was constant danger from other criminals and the police, which is why he used random mini-cabs, and why he never got dropped off exactly where he was going. He liked to check the area out first, making sure he wasn't under surveillance from another firm or Old Bill. But, for Vinnie, sometimes all this Secret Squirrel shit was a pain in the arse. 'Come on then, let's walk.'

After a few strides Sean suddenly stopped and put a hand on Vinnie's shoulder. He was staring down the left-hand side of Cricklewood Broadway. 'Are you on this?' he asked, quietly.

Vinnie looked in the same direction as Sean and saw the white security van parked outside the Allied Irish. The Broadway was quiet after the bustle of the day and before the hardcore night people came out to play. This was the golden hour when the streets and pavements are reasonably empty and even footsteps seem to echo through the warm concrete passageways of the big city.

Vinnie squinted. 'I bet they're filling the cashpoints,' he said, thoughtfully.

Sean smiled, his blue eyes twinkling under the streetlight.

'Tis a feckin sign from the gods!' said Sean in an exaggerated Irish accent as he poked Vinnie lightly in the chest.

Vinnie shook his head. 'You can't be fucking serious?'

Sean nodded. 'Why not?'

Vinnie spread his hands as if what he was saying should be quite obvious. 'Why not? Are you fucking off-key, or what? We're dressed in fucking monkey suits, we've no tools or masks with us, and... well...'

Sean walked quickly to a nearby litter bin. He picked up a brown paper McDonalds bag and emptied cold fries and cardboard containers from it. He rooted deeper into the bin and pulled out an empty plastic carrier bag. He ripped a couple of holes in the paper bag and put it over his head. The eye-holes weren't quite on the money so Sean adjusted and made the holes bigger.

'You know you look like fucking SpongeBob Square-Pants?' Vinnie said, and then shook his head in resignation and began rooting in the next bin along the street.

Meanwhile, Sean found a wine bottle in a shop doorway.

Inside the Allied Irish Bank, the guards had finished loading bank notes into two of the four cash machines. They had relaxed slightly, and the only sounds they could hear were the ripping of the plastic packets and the slight solid thump as they slotted the thick bundles of notes into the open machines. The street outside seemed quiet; nothing out of the ordinary. They now had to pick up two more cases of cash from the van. They stood inside the door and scanned the street for anything unusual. It was all clear. The first guard unlocked the door and they stepped out onto the street.

The custodian in the back of the security van couldn't see much from his position by the safe. There was a narrow strip of a window at head-height, which allowed him to see the section of pavement in front of the bank and the front door. He watched his two colleagues step out from the bank and up to the side-hatch on the van. Two bangs on the side of the van was the signal for two cash bags. He pulled two hard-plastic cash cases from the large on-board safe. Each case contained a canvas cash bag containing bundles of plastic-wrapped bank notes. He put the first case into the cash chute and waited for the guard outside to remove it and shut the chute door. He then placed the second case into the chute and pushed it through.

The two guards were almost at the bank door when their world was suddenly turned upside down. 'GET ON THE FUCKING GROUND! NOW!'

The voices were loud and very aggressive. The first guard was body-slammed by a large man in what appeared to be a suit and tie but wearing a paper bag on his head. He hit the ground hard and lost his grip on the cash box, which set off the alarm in the box. A loud whooping screech started coming from the box. It could only be stopped by the guard turning his personal alarm key anti-clockwise in the lock. The man who had knocked him down was now standing over him pointing what appeared to be a long gun wrapped in a white plastic bag. The guard could see a pair of intense blue eyes boring into him, but the rest of the man's face was obscured by the paper bag he was using as a mask.

'TURN THE FUCKING ALARM OFF! DO IT NOW!'

The robber's voice was muffled by his makeshift mask, but the guard heard every word. He scrabbled at the keyring on his belt and managed to find the long brass alum key that killed the alarm. In the relative silence, the guard became aware of a second masked man, this one wearing a Sainsbury's carrier bag with holes ripped into it for eyes. He, too, was carrying a gun wrapped in a newspaper. The second robber had the second guard up against the side of the van with the paper-wrapped gun next to his temple.

'OPEN THE BOXES!' The first robber jabbed his gun into the guard's face as he shouted. The guard knew this was no time for heroics – these men meant business. He quickly fitted the key and opened the box, revealing the cash bag inside. The robber snatched the canvas money bag and jabbed his weapon towards the guard's face. 'NOW FACE DOWN, OR I'LL BLOW YOUR FUCKING HEAD CLEAN OFF!'

And then... silence. The guard risked lifting his head from the pavement and looking around. He could see his mate, sitting on the ground, legs splayed out and back leaning against the wheel of the security van. He looked devastated by what had just happened; shell-shocked. The guard unclipped his personal radio and keyed the mic. 'Oscar Tango Two, Oscar Tango Two...' he croaked. 'Code Red. Repeat. We've got a Code Red...'

Two streets away, Sean and Vinnie Bradish were loping along at a steady pace, laughing loudly as they fled with £86,000 in stolen cash.

The Bradish boys had struck again.

CHAPTER FOUR

YOUNG GUNS

Since the arrest and imprisonment of Jimmy Doyle's gang in the previous year, the remnants of the Dirty Dozen gang had been running wild and leaving their mark all over London. Sean and Vincent Bradish, Stephen Roberts, Steven Hall, Black Tony and Danny Mac had been robbing and pillaging the capital's banking institutions at will. Sean and Vinnie Bradish had been the newest members of Doyle's gang and learned their trade by engaging in robberies planned by the 'Ayatollah'. They were lucky enough not to be scooped up with the rest of the gang on that fateful summer morning in 1995 and, with most of the major players in prison, or taking retirement to go straight for a while – or, in Doyle's case, on the run – Sean and Vinnie found themselves at the head of this loose criminal organisation.

They had access to plenty of firearms, they had the brains and bottle to carry on where Doyle had been rudely interrupted and they had no qualms about doing it. Sean was a natural leader and the rest of the gang, including his older brother Vinnie, accepted him as such. Sean had very little fear in him and kept a cool head under pressure. Stephen Roberts was a car-theft expert who could steal almost any car to order. He was scared of Sean but knew at the same time that Sean was a money-getter, and the only thing Roberts liked more than Class A drugs was money. Vincent 'Vinnie' Bradish was the more relaxed and easy-going brother, a good planner who enjoyed organising a job and spending the money. Steven Hall and Black Tony were old friends of Stephen Roberts, Hall being his best friend. Danny Mac was a hanger-on who could be relied on in a pinch. He would let the gang store guns at his flat and sometimes drive gang members about on errands. Then there were other characters who would team up with the gang for specific robberies, but the Bradish brothers and Roberts were the nucleus of the revamped Dirty Dozen.

The gang had hit a couple of Thomas Cook shops under Doyle's instructions, and knew exactly how easy they were to rob and how much ready cash they held. So they engaged on a campaign to rob as many of them as they could. Their plan was simple and very close to the template introduced to them by Jimmy Doyle. Two men would go into the premises, armed, masked and gloved, and, within a couple of minutes, they would exit with the foreign reserve and whatever sterling they were holding. Ideally, they would get behind the security counters by threatening cashiers to open the doors and then rob the safe, if it was open, because most of the Thomas Cook shop safes were on timers that would not allow them to be opened straight away. Failing that, they would clear out the cash drawers, stealing foreign currency, traveller's cheques and sterling from the cashiers. This was a good payday, netting between £10,000 and £50,000 a time.

Once the money started flying in, the boys would spend it on cars – BMWs, Audis and Jaguars – or high-powered motorbikes, designer clothes and holidays. They were truly living the good life, and Stephen Roberts started to use more and more cocaine. His gram on 'special occasions' turned into a £200-a-day habit very quickly and his life, which had never been very structured, became even more erratic. When the gang had successfully pulled off a robbery their habit was to buy a new set of designer clothes and party throughout the night. Roberts, though, started to make excuses not to go out with the gang.

Vinnie told me, 'After we'd had a good one over, we'd be off out for a few drinks on the manor, you know, put a bit of the money back into the local community. But not Roberts. He'd make excuses, like he had to take his bird out or he'd arranged a meet with someone. I used to say to Sean, "There's something dodgy about that fella," but Sean wouldn't have it.'

The revamped Dirty Dozen gang were hitting one or sometimes two or three targets a month in order to fund their lifestyles and also, it has to be said, because they enjoyed the excitement of the life. Due to their prolific work rate, they soon came to the attention of Finchley Flying Squad and would often catch sight of plain-clothes police watching and following them. To the gang, it was a funny game, keeping ahead of the police. Sometimes Vinnie would be leaving his house on his motorbike and would wave to the undercover officers watching him and mouth, 'See you later.' Both the Bradish brothers were skilful bikers and could easily outrun or outmanoeuvre police vehicles. Whenever the gang went to commit a robbery, they would spend a lot of time on anti-surveillance actions, doubling back on themselves, driving down dead-end roads and circling roundabouts until anyone following them would be as dizzy as a schoolgirl.

They were stealing a lot of cash but spending it just as quickly. A lot of people think that all bank robbers are ultra-smart people who will invest their ill-gotten gains and just live off the profits for the rest of their lives, but this is usually far from the truth. Most robbers do not trust banking organisations because they can see how easy it is to rob them, and they fear that their own money can just as easily be reached by the authorities for compensation if they are convicted. The robbers creed of 'spend it fast or they might get it back' was paramount with the Bradish gang. These were guys who had grown up in poverty and who knew that money, if you ever got hold of any, was for spending. Nobody really cared about the future; it was right now that counted. As far as they were concerned, there was an inevitability in getting nicked and spending decades behind bars or being shot dead on the street by a police bullet. It was the game they were in. I'm not saying that they did any deep thinking and philosophising about such matters but, if you take up the gun for a living, you know that you are playing for high stakes if you win, and also if you lose. It is constantly in the back of your mind.

The new version of the Dirty Dozen were hitting so many targets that the Flying Squad were seriously interested in them. The thing was, Under Jimmy Doyle's leadership, the gang had followed his personal plan, which meant that it had taken years for the Flying Squad to actually get any idea that all of these robberies were being committed by the same gang. However, the new version of the Dirty Dozen were hitting so many targets in a short space of time that the Flying Squad took an active interest in them almost from day one.

Under the leadership of Sean Bradish, it was more of a free-for-all. He thought that what they were doing was more akin to chaos; striking out of the blue, not really making detailed plans for most jobs and just robbing any target that happened to take their fancy. And through this chaos, Sean was hoping the police could find no foothold of evidence or suspicion to help them arrest the gang. But what they were really doing was falling into a routine that was bound to be spotted by experienced officers of the Flying Squad.

The gang developed certain habits that were just as tell-tale as the police knowing that a Vauxhall Astra getaway car was the hallmark sign of a Jimmy Doyle robbery. Sean had a penchant for baseball caps and bandannas, so these became the gang's go-to disguises. A lot of robbers will wear ski-masks on robberies as the only bit of their face that would be on view to public and CCTV cameras will be a bit of skin around the eyes and mouth. Bandannas offer no such protection from recognition. It's true that a bandanna on the lower part of the face, along with a hood, can be enough to put doubt in the mind of a jury but, with the improved quality of CCTV images, it would still enable a police officer to hazard an intelligent guess as to who it is. Not enough for a conviction but enough for recognition, and sometimes that is all the police need to mount an operation.

Sean and Vinnie could never really take the threat of the Flying Squad seriously. They operated for nearly five years knowing that they were being intermittently followed and watched by the police, but were never even arrested or questioned by them. As Vinnie commented:

These Flying Squad are supposed to be the elite, the top boys at what they do, but, as far as I was concerned, they were fucking fools. The amount of times they could have just stepped in and nicked us red-handed over them years was almost unbelievable. We were in more danger of getting our collars felt by traffic cops than from the Flying Squad.

Despite the fact that it is well known that the Flying Squad like to nick their perps while actually engaged in the act of armed robbery, it is still hard to work out why they allowed the gang to get away with so much for so long. Vinnie – and Sean to a certain extent – is convinced that Stephen Roberts was the reason. Their theory is that Roberts was in bed with the police even before he was brought into the gang, and that he was directed to get in with the gang and report back to his police handlers. Vinnie sees it as being something along the lines of the Johnny Depp/Al Pacino movie *Donnie Brasco*, where Depp's character, an undercover cop, is set up to join the mafia as a member in order to bring the organisation down from the inside. In the movie, Depp becomes so involved with the bad guys, some of whom he grows to like and respect, that he starts to enjoy the lifestyle and spins it out as long as he can. Vinnie thinks that this is what happened to Roberts. But the Dirty Dozen were no mafia organisation and Stephen Roberts was definitely no Johnny Depp.

Whatever was to happen in later years, for now, in the late 1990s, everything was going great for the Dirty Dozen. The gang were living the life and living it well.

CHAPTER FIVE

THOMAS COOK: THE GIFT THAT KEPT ON GIVING

The Bradish boys, just like other armed-robbery gangs who were in the know, targeted the premises of the travel agents Thomas Cook. It might seem like an unlikely target to the general public – why would you rob a travel agency when there are thousands of banks, building societies and Post Offices holding large sums of cash? Well, the answer is quite simple: up until relatively recently, the large sums of cash held by Thomas Cook travel agencies were not known, except by the company itself and a select few armed-robbery gangs around the country, and it is a hell of a lot easier to rob a travel agency than institutions with decades of experience of being robbed.

Up until the 1970s, blaggers looked in the obvious places for their bit of work – all the premises mentioned above, as well as jewellery shops, supermarkets and cinemas. Nobody except rank amateurs would rob shops unconnected to cash or valuables – it just wasn't worth the candle. Robbing shops was the sort of game that youngsters would try when they were just starting out in a life of serious crime. The trouble with robbing shops was that your take would be minimal – usually whatever they had in the tills – and your prison sentence would be heavy if caught and convicted. The average prison sentence for the armed robbery of a shop would be between five and twelve years and, when you think that robbing a bank would mean a bigger cash prize, with maybe a couple more years added to your sentence, it makes sense to go for the more lucrative target.

The average bank robbery can net anything from £500 to £50,000, depending on a lot of factors: whether you hit the tills or are lucky enough to get an open vault, the time of day, the amount of daily business they do, whether there has been a recent cash delivery, among other things. Without inside information, robbing a high-street bank is like purchasing a lottery ticket – you pay your money and hope for the best. As I mentioned in a previous chapter, the Wembley Bank Robbers were taking the present-day equivalent of hundreds of thousands of pounds out of high-street banks, and every bank robber since has been hoping for the same kind of paydays, but sometimes you end up with nish. I, personally, have been on bank robberies that netted absolutely zero prize – nothing. In those circumstances, it pays to be a realist. You shrug your shoulders and you walk away, knowing there were thousands of other targets out there that would be lucrative. By nature, I believe a lot of serious criminals are not only actors but also pragmatists. You cannot take it personally.

So what were these other targets? Well, building societies were easy but held less money than banks; Post Offices were hit-and-miss because, on the whole, the subs were family-run, and families can be hard to deal with in a quick and dangerous situation; jewellery shops were great, but then you had the bother of fencing out the goods, which meant third parties involved and little cash on the spot – you would have to sell on the 'tom' and wait for the money. Not an ideal situation, particularly for impatient thieves, which, by definition, most armed robbers are. Armed robbers are 'Now!' people. They don't want to go to work and save for years to get that new car or have to put the pennies away for a year to be able to afford a holiday; they want it NOW! As I say, greedy, lazy bastards with little patience.

In the late 1990s, there was a little firm of armed robbers reaving in London, led by a Scotsman called 'Gussy', who stumbled onto the fact that Thomas Cook travel shops were holding huge amounts of ready cash. They quickly rinsed as many Thomas Cooks as they could and found themselves rolling in money. Flash new cars, penthouse flats and plenty of blingy tom followed. Unfortunately, a bit of professional jealousy soured this little team and they ended up fighting among themselves. Gussy was thrown out of a third-floor window by some of his associates and very nearly died. His injuries were so serious that he was given the Last Rites. In the event, he recovered from his injuries just in time to receive an eighteen-year sentence for armed robbery after the firm was nicked and convicted.

But the effect that the Gussy gang had on the armed-robbery fraternity once they reached prison was almost incendiary. In prison there is a little-known (to the public) but very dangerous practice of 'showing your deps' to other prisoners. Let me explain. If you are sent to trial in the UK and you will be pleading 'not guilty', you will be sent the depositions concerning the case you are accused of. In the deposition bundle will be everything you need to know about the accusations that have been levelled against you, all the written statements of the witnesses, the police and the victims, photographic evidence, a list of all exhibits and the location they were found, and all of your call logs from phones. This is to allow you to present a case to the jury answering the accusations. For many years now, deposition bundles have been shared by like-minded criminals as 'textbooks' of further criminal education. If you want to know how much cash is held in, say, Barclays bank tills, or the security routine of the Halifax Building Society, or the name of the head cashier at a branch of HSBC, you can find all of this info in the deps of an armed robber.

Armed robbers are, mainly, serious career criminals and, whether you like it or not, they hold a bit of a 'special status' in prison. In the land of prison, where 90 per cent of the inhabitants are serving time for petty offending, armed robbers are viewed as a criminal elite – they go after the big prizes and have to accept huge prison sentences when they are captured. In prison, they gravitate towards others like themselves and, usually, are given a wide berth by other prisoners. Personal rivalries notwithstanding, jailed armed robbers will pool information about future possible targets and scout out other robbers who have 'specialist' knowledge in their deps. So the armed robber's deposition bundle is a compendium of goodies that actually helps to further their careers. Nice one, CPS.

I must mention that armed robbers are not the only ones who share their deps in prison. It has been well documented that sex offenders – and paedophiles, in particular – will share each other's deposition, but not necessarily for the technical knowledge that they might glean from the pages. They use the pages as a sick kind of pornography.

So, when Gussy's gang landed on the jailhouse floor, they started handing the deps around to a chosen few. Suddenly, Thomas Cook shops shot straight to the top of the armed robbers' target list. The reason for so much ready cash on these premises was not only due to the fact that people were paying for their holidays, but because Thomas Cook also housed a money exchange in almost every shop. They held large amounts of foreign currency in their safes – dollars, euros, yen, etc. – and their security was laughable. In most cases, their surveillance cameras, if fitted at all, were of poor quality and out of date, so the pictures could not be used as evidence or to identify a suspect. When the armed robbers read about this, it was open season on every branch of Thomas Cook in the country. The first incarnation of the Dirty Dozen gang started robbing Thomas Cook branches under the leadership of Jimmy Doyle. The Bradish boys had already stolen some very tidy sums of cash from a couple of branches at Doyle's direction. Now it was their turn and they were not going to be slow at coming forward.

CHAPTER SIX

ON THE PAVEMENT

The first robbery that Steven Roberts carried out with the Bradish brothers was on a Thomas Cook travel agency, which was not surprising as the police estimate that Sean Bradish robbed at least twenty-two Thomas Cook branches during his robbery career. Roberts was both impressed by and a little frightened of Sean Bradish. After seeing his antics with a suspected rapist, where Sean had ruined the man's face with a pint glass, Roberts was in no doubt that Sean was capable of serving up some severe violence to anyone who crossed him. Roberts own criminal past proved he was no snowflake when it came to dishing out the cosh, but always when he was in control and the victims were easy meat. He could be ruthless, up to a point, but the odds had to be in his favour. He knew the Bradish brothers were money-getters and top of their game, and he wanted in. He put his fear to one side and agreed to go along on a robbery with them.

The Thomas Cook shop on Kilburn Road was typical of its type – big glass front windows covered in brightly coloured cards and posters advertising cheap holiday bargains. Inside were four open-plan desks where the staff could deal with customers, and up at the back wall was a bank-type counter with bullet-proof screens and three tills. Behind the counter were two cashiers who would deal with any customers wanting to buy foreign currency. There was a medium-sized safe behind the counter, which held shelves of crisp foreign bank notes as well as bundles of UK currency. The atmosphere inside the shop was quiet and peaceful.

Two customers, a middle-aged white couple, sat in front of one of the open-plan desks looking through glossy holiday brochures. They were attended by the shop's manager, a dark-haired, smartly dressed woman in her thirties. There was one other female member of staff busily perusing her computer screen behind the first desk as you come through the door. It was 10.15 on a bright Thursday morning in May.

Half a mile away from the Thomas Cook shop, three men sat quietly in a black BMW 5 Series. The car had been stolen from a train-station car park in Buckinghamshire a week previously. It had been boosted by Steven Roberts who, despite his many other failings, was an expert car thief. He had opened the door of the car by inserting the blade of a large pair of medical scissors into the lock and jiggling it. Once the door lock had been sprung, the alarm automatically sounded. The loud whooping of the car alarm was of no consequence to Roberts; he had stolen many cars in his life and had found that most people ignored the sound of alarms (unless they are fire alarms) in the daylight hours, as they assume they have been set off accidently. An alarm in the dead of night has the power to galvanise people into action – alarms are scary in the dark – but, in daylight, they lose some of the power to alarm.

Roberts jumped into the vehicle and pulled a slide-hammer from inside his jacket. He screwed the self-tapping screw into the ignition lock until it was in tight, then gripped the heavyweight slide handle of the tool and jerked it hard. The lock was stubborn, and he had to jerk the slide twice more before the whole ignition lock popped out of its barrel. Once the lock had been removed, Roberts stuck a large flathead screwdriver into the vandalised barrel and twisted it. The alarm stopped dead and, in the relative silence, the engine fired up and purred nicely. Roberts drove calmly away.

The three men now waiting in that stolen BMW included Roberts, Sean Bradish and Vinnie Bradish. Sean had picked up on a strong rumour about the amount of cash held at Thomas Cook and decided it was time the gang stepped in and got their share. They had picked a target on the manor for their first sortie. Vinnie, who was more of a planner than most in the gang, had checked the layout of the target, how many staff on duty, walked the getaway route and noted all CCTV in the area. Vinnie had decided that the optimum time to hit the target was mid-morning, just after the cash delivery had been made.

Sean was in the front passenger seat, Roberts in the

driver's seat and Vinnie was in the back seat behind Roberts. All three were scanning the area while not seeming to.

'What tools did you bring?' asked Vinnie. Sean took care of all the weapons and chose what they would use for each job. The gang had a large number of guns, including a .44 Magnum revolver, a couple of World War II Webley pistols, .22 pistols, a Colt .38 snub-nose, a .225 Derringer and several sawn-off shotguns, including a Savage 5-shot pump-action. Sean did love a gun.

Sean rooted about in the green holdall between his feet. He pulled out a sawn-off 16-gauge Stevens shotgun with black masking tape around the stock and handed it to Vinnie. Vinnie expertly flicked open the barrels and checked the bright brass ends of the birdshot cartridges. Satisfied, he swung the barrels shut with a satisfying thunk. Sean then passed a long-barrelled .22 target pistol to Roberts, who stuck it inside his jean jacket. For himself, Sean had the Colt Python magnum, a fearsome-looking gun capable of blowing a hole the size of a grapefruit in whatever it hit.

Vinnie had no intention of shooting anyone; he just wanted the prize and for it to be over. He'd much rather be drinking a few pints with the lads than hanging around Kilburn with a loaded gun in his coat. He loved the life he was living, the absolute freedom, the money, cars, drink and women, but he wasn't enamoured with the actual robberies. Sean, on the other hand, had the real bug; he'd go out robbing on his own just for the fun of it. He believed it was his calling and, to Sean, committing these sorts of crimes was much more addictive than any Class A drugs he could buy with the proceeds. He was buzzing.

Roberts took a packet of chewing gum out of his pocket and offered it round. There were no takers. He was still a bit jittery from the previous night's cocktail of mind-altering drugs and his mouth was as dry as an Arab's sandal. He didn't really fancy doing this robbery but he needed the money, so needs must, but he was always nervous before a job.

Vinnie cleared his throat. 'Right,' he said, 'there should be no more than four oul ones in the gaff, don't know how many customers so we'll have to play that by ear. Sean, you know what to do. Steve, just stay by the door and make sure nobody gets out before we do. Are we right?'

Sean nodded, a small smile on his face, he was about to be in his element. Roberts swallowed hard and pulled his baseball cap low over his eyes. In his mind he was repeating the word 'Fuck!' on a continuous loop, trying to block out the bowel-watering fear he now had. The three men exited the car in an unhurried fashion. Sean straightened his jacket and adjusted for the weight of the Colt in his waistband.

The three robbers split up and made their way around to the target in single file, senses switched to high alert as their eyes scanned the surrounding area for anything out of the ordinary that might lead them to suspect a 'ready eye'*. The police have a penchant for ambushing armed robbers during, or just after, the commission of the crime. In the 1980s and 1990s, the Flying Squad and PT17 (the then firearms squad) had shot dead many seasoned armed robbers on the streets, so it became *de rigeur* for robbers to be ultra-alert around their target.

The reason the police did this was because so many of the armed robbers that they had arrested in the past were found not guilty at court. If they were arrested before committing the job, they would hire the best QCs in the country and put forward a story as to why they happened to be sitting in a car full of guns and masks. This was around the time when the many and egregious police fit-ups of the 1970s were coming to the fore as major miscarriages of justice amid conflagrations of publicity. In short, as far as juries (i.e. the general public) were concerned, the police could not be trusted to tell the truth. So the Flying Squad changed their MO and decided a dead robber was better than a not-guilty robber. Their favourite trick was now to catch robbers leaving a just-committed robbery, still (preferably) with the guns in their hands. The fact is that, in this situation, they knew it was likely that the robbers would put up resistance so the police would be ready, guns in hand. As a result, a proportion of armed robbers were put down.

To Stephen Roberts, every single thing he spotted had his nerves jumping and jangling. An old woman pulling a shopping trolley – Old Bill! A blind man tapping down the pavement with his white-stick – Old Bill! Two schoolboys waiting outside a sweet-shop – Old Bill! If Roberts had the courage, he knew he would drop out of this job right now. He didn't trust Sean. He had witnessed the savage violence that Sean dished out to anyone who crossed him, and he had no wish to be on the receiving end. But he loved money, and he was way too lazy to go and do a day's work. Roberts was a veteran of violent thefts and robberies, but on a smaller scale than this and when he was in charge. He trailed the Bradish brothers along the pavement, fingering the .22 pistol in his pocket, and tried to think of the money they would steal.

Sean glanced around for the last time and slipped his bandanna over the lower half of his face just outside the entrance to Thomas Cook. Vinnie and Roberts followed suit. Sean pushed his way into the premises, pulling his gun from his waistband as he moved. It was peaceful on the premises; the murmur of conversation was low and there was a soft shuffling sound as bank notes whizzed through a note-counting machine behind the till counter.

'Now then...' Sean's gruff voice was loud and commanding. Everyone on the premises looked towards the three figures who had just entered. They saw three masked men with what seemed like large and menacing firearms. Roberts stayed by the door, stepping from one foot to another in a nervous fashion and swivelling the .22 pistol in all directions. Sean was in control, the adrenalin buzzing and popping like champagne through his veins. He gripped the Colt with both hands in a shooter's stance, knees slightly bent and his bright-blue eyes staring straight down the barrel. He moved the gun steadily, pointing it at each person in turn in order to let them know who was in control.

Vinnie weaved quickly between the open-plan desks,

the shotgun held down at his waist in one hand with the barrels pointing at the floor. He wasn't worried about the staff or customers trying anything; Sean had them covered. He was almost casual in his actions. He took a folded plastic bag from the pocket of his army-surplus jacket and threw it onto the counter in front of the cashiers.

'Start sticking the notes in there, love,' he said. 'And NO dye-packs, or I'll paint these walls RED!'

One of the cashiers pulled the plastic bag under the screen and started putting handfuls of bank notes from the till into it. The second cashier began to unlock her till. Over by the door, Roberts was getting panicky. He was breathing heavily and his eyes, above the bandanna that covered the lower part of his face, were bulging. 'Come on... come on...' He muttered. He was observing the street outside as if expecting the police to roll up any minute.

Sean waved his gun at the two customers and the staff and ordered them to sit on the floor.

'Nobody do anything silly and nobody will get hurt,' he said, loudly. The only sound in the room now was Roberts' loud breathing and the busy sounds of bank notes hitting the bottom of the bag. Vinnie watched as the first cashier emptied her till into the bag, then he gestured for her to pass it to her mate. The second cashier took up the task.

Sean glanced at his watch. 'One minute,' he shouted towards Vinnie. 'And get the safe as well.'

In reality, their robberies were not timed affairs; they took as long as they took. But their average was around four minutes to clear the cash from a target. The performance with the watch was nothing but a bit of theatre; a nod towards the heist films that the brothers had grown up watching. Behind his mask, Sean was grinning.

Vinnie watched as a blue canvas sack of cash was released from the small safe behind the counter by the second cashier. 'That's the stuff!' he said, happily. His plastic bag, now bulging with cash, was pushed through the hatch. Vinnie snatched it from the counter and was gratified to feel the weight of the prize. He told the two cashiers to lay face-down on the floor. Their time here was just about done.

Sean gestured to Roberts. 'Out,' he said. Roberts didn't need telling twice. He slipped the long-barrelled pistol inside his coat and turned to the door, pulling his bandanna from his face as he stepped from the premises. The cold air on his face chilled the sweat on his forehead and upper lip. Coming outside after such an intense four minutes was surreal. The world suddenly seemed to be full of sound and motion, car engines, voices and colours. It was like switching from slow, quiet, black and white into full colour surround sound instantly.

Sean, still in the premises, stood stock still and allowed Vinnie to pass him and get out of the door with the prize. He moved the gun slowly over the scene in a menacing manner before stepping up to the door. As he exited, he suddenly felt a cold liquid spraying over him from a device above the door. He stopped dead in the doorway.

The device above the door was a security innovation that could be operated from behind the counter and it contained Smart Water, an indelible infra-red liquid dye. When sprayed at armed robbers, it could stain the clothing and skin for weeks, allowing the police to run an infra-red light over any suspect and know if they were the guilty party. Each batch of Smart Water contained a DNA marking that was unique to each premises. Sean knew what had been sprayed at him and he also knew that it could only have been operated by one of the cashiers behind the counter. This incensed him.

His eyes blazing, he strode back into the premises and up to the counter. He pointed the large handgun at both cashiers, who were by now hugging each other in terror. He stood in front of the bullet-proof screen, pointing his gun directly at the heads of the two cashiers.

'Who done that?' he said, menacingly. 'Who fucking did it?'

Neither of the cashiers answered. They just clutched each other tighter and whimpered, terrified that this madman was going to shoot them dead.

Sean banged a fist on the counter, rattling the frame. 'Who did it?'

Outside on the pavement, Vinnie had realised that his brother was not with him. He quickly turned on his heel and pushed his way back into the premises. He saw Sean, heard his words, and knew that his brother was in one of his white rages, where nothing else mattered except what he was focused on. Vinnie quickly made his way up to the counter and stepped right in front of Sean. He glared into his eyes, almost a mirror of his own but with a more deadly intent, and spoke through gritted teeth.

'Rein it in, now,' Vinnie snarled. 'Time to go. Old Bill are on their way.'

Vinnie's words seemed to hit home, and he saw some of the rage shift behind his brother's eyes. For a moment, Vinnie thought he might have to give him a sharp crack with the barrel of his gun to get him moving but Sean suddenly turned on his heel and headed unhurriedly for the exit.

'Don't ever do that to me again,' were Sean's parting words, dripping with threat and menace. And then the robbers were gone, the door slowly closing on their exit. Inside Thomas Cook, there suddenly began a crying and keening sound from the relieved but traumatised staff and customers.

Outside on the street, Sean and Vinnie, guns now hidden and bandannas removed, walked at a brisk pace towards the getaway car. Roberts was already in the driving seat, drumming his fingers on the steering wheel and chewing gum impatiently. If he wasn't so desperate for his share of the proceeds, he would have driven off and left the brothers in the lurch. He twisted the screwdriver in the ignition as the Bradish boys jumped into the car. Vinnie put a hand on Robert's shoulder. 'Take it easy now,' he said. 'None of that motor-racing shit. Just pull away as though we're as innocent as the day is long.'

The haul from the first robbery committed by Roberts with the Bradish boys was £26,000. Just over eight grand a piece. Some of it was in foreign bank notes, but they were easy to change into English money. They had been inside the premises for under four minutes. Stephen Roberts was buzzing.

THE MAGIC OF SUFFERINGS

CHAPTER SEVEN

THE MAKING OF A SUPERGRASS

It has been well documented that the template for the modern-day bank robbery was set back in 1867, in Clay County, Missouri, by the James-Younger Gang. A bunch of ex-confederate 'bushwhackers', bitter from losing the civil war (1861–65) and broke, they decided that the most direct route to getting compensation from the Union was by walking into their banks in broad daylight and holding firearms on the staff and customers before clearing out the tills and vault. The gang were the first to do this and their innovation helped them to steal the equivalent in today's currency of over five million dollars. The gang's leader was the infamous Jesse James.

Fast-forward to the UK in the late 1960s and we can see that the in-through-the-front-door method of armed robbery pioneered by the James-Younger Gang is still very much in vogue. London has become the robbery capital of the world, with an average of three armed raids per week, and the villains are coining it. High in the premiere league of armed raiders are the infamous Wembley Mob, a gang of criminals and gunmen who have perfected the Jesse James template and refined it for the modern era. Known originally as The Crash-Bang Gang because of their method of entry – they would drive a car up onto the pavement outside a bank, kick the doors open and fire a shot into the ceiling in order to focus everyone's attention. The gang included smart, hardened robbers such as Micky 'the Pimpernel' Green and the soon-to-be-infamous Derek Creighton Smalls, also known as 'Bertie'.

They became known as the Wembley Mob when, in the summer of 1972, the gang took less than three minutes to rob £138,000 in cash from the Wembley branch of Barclays Bank. By this time, there was an armed robbery committed, on average, every five days in London and, since 1969, over three million pounds had been stolen at gunpoint. West London was fast becoming the Wild West. The Wembley Mob robbed vast amounts of money and jewellery from banks, counting houses and jewellery makers, and would jet off to Torremolinos straight after the robberies. It was during this period that the blaggers mantra became 'sawn-off shotguns on the streets of London at lunchtime, sawn-off shorts on the beach in Spain at teatime.' But the salad days do not last forever and the Wembley Mob were about to get the rudest of awakenings.

'Bertie' Smalls was said to have been the most ruthless and violent member of the Wembley Mob. He would not hesitate to shoot anyone who got in his way. But he was also a very cunning man, who would stop at nothing to preserve his own liberty. When he was arrested straight after a £10,000 robbery at a bank in Palmers Green, Bertie decided to lighten his own load by putting the weight on his mates. He agreed to turn Queen's Evidence on his compatriots, to give evidence about all of his own crimes and theirs, in return for freedom. Smalls was the first major robber to turn QE, and the repercussions were still being felt around the criminal world many years later. On his evidence, twenty-seven men were convicted and jailed for a combined total of 322 years.

The only person, apart from Smalls himself, to benefit from this action was a small-time criminal named Jimmy Saunders, who had been well and truly fitted up by the police and the infamously corrupt DI Bert Wickstead. Saunders had been convicted of taking part in the 1970 raid on Barclays Bank in Ilford, which had netted £237,000 in cash, and he had been sentenced to twelve years in prison. When Smalls turned over his confederates, he gave up every detail, and one of those details was that Saunders, despite police 'evidence' to the contrary, was never on the Ilford bank robbery. If the police and the Director of Public Prosecutions were going to use Smalls statements to convict others and claim what he said was true, Saunders had to be released.

Jimmy Saunders was probably the only man left in the criminal underworld with a good word to say about Bertie Smalls but, if he did say anything, he must have whispered. Bertie Smalls had become the first supergrass and opened the door for any future ruthless and violent criminals who didn't fancy doing the time, even though they had committed the crime.

Giving evidence against your mates became known as 'doing a Bertie', and the fact that Smalls managed to walk away scot-free meant no comeback from the law. His criminal confederates were not so forgiving, and a very lucrative 'contract' was put on his head by those he had betrayed. He died of natural causes decades later, but his betrayal and escape sent a seismic shift through the underworld. After Smalls came a succession of so-called hardened criminals, like rats crawling out of a sewer, who were willing and able to throw their friends and associates under a bus for a sniff of freedom. Only Smalls was able to parlay his information into a no-prison deal, and the DPP decided that the deal was really too distasteful to ever repeat.

It was decided that, after Smalls, other supergrasses would have to at least get a nominal sentence in order to make it look like justice was being done. The 'supergrass tariff' – i.e. the prison sentence they would be given – was set at between five and eight years. But this was no hardship to the would-be informers, as it was made clear to them that their time would not be spent in the filthy and brutal prison system surrounded by the men they had betrayed; no, they would serve their time in secret police-station cells with all the comforts of home, including conjugal visits, meals ordered in and plenty of fags and booze. They would also be granted parole and time off for good behaviour at the earliest possible opportunity. It became such a great wheeze for these men that some of them went on to turn supergrass more than once.

Another of the Wembley Mob who followed Bertie Smalls into the witness box was Don 'Crazy Horse' Barrett. Barrett had been the only one arrested after a Bournemouth bank robbery and was jailed for twelve years. While in prison, he heard about the antics of Smalls and immediately put himself forward as a supergrass. Unfortunately for Barrett, Smalls had already shot his load and a lot of the stuff he had given the police was the same as what Barrett wanted to give. There is no doubt that Don Barrett had fallen out with the gang, and felt that he had been abandoned to his fate as the only one arrested and convicted of the Bournemouth bank job. It is said that some of the gang had threatened his girlfriend, but the main reason Barrett came forward was to escape his prison sentence. In the end, the DPP did not use any of Barrett's statements. It turns out he was the first supergrass to be made redundant. So 'Crazy Horse' returned to prison to serve his twelve-year sentence, never guessing that his day would come again in the future.

After his release, Barrett went back to criminality, though his reputation had taken something of a dent when news of his indiscretions hit the criminal world. A lot of people did not trust him – and rightly so – but there were always minor-league villains willing to overlook such stains on a person's character as long as he is a money-getter. It was not until 1985 that Don 'Crazy Horse' Barrett made it back into the premiere league of villainy. And that was all down to a man named David Croke.

David Croke was a clever and ruthless individual who had been on the fringes of criminality all of his life. Although, on the surface, he was a respectable citizen with his own business, living in the suburbs of north London in a house called Emerald, underneath he was a master planner who decided, at a fairly late stage of his life, to go balls-out and become an armed robber. Dave loved the planning aspect of armed robbery and would sometimes spend months following cash-in-transit vehicles in order to work out their routes. He would use disguises and a variety of cars. Dave had studied the art of armed robbery for years and his aim was to come up with a fool-proof method of stealing large amounts of cash. He figured that, if he followed the same van every couple of weeks, he would know every stop on its route. Therefore, he could work out the best place to hit the target for maximum pay-out. But Dave was in need of a heavy; someone with practical experience of armed robbery. And this is where Don Barrett enters stage left.

Dave was introduced to Barrett by a mutual criminal friend who told him, on the quiet, that Barrett had attempted to go supergrass back in the 1970s. This friend was, in fact, a well-known villain called George Ince. Ince had married Dolly Kray, Charlie Kray's ex-wife. He was assured that Barrett had 'pretended' to turn supergrass in order to get out of jail, and that he was a staunch robber. Dave spoke to one of his mates, Tommy Wisbey, one of the Great Train Robbers, about Barrett and was told that he was a 'good worker' and was asked incredulously, 'What are the chances of him going supergrass a second time?'

Everyone agreed that Barrett would be 'safe' to work with, so Dave took a chance. He was to regret it for the rest of his life.

One of the ideas that Dave Croke had come up with was to convince his wife's son, Alan Turner, who had no previous convictions, to get a job as a custodian for an armoured-van company called Shield Security. Once ensconced in the company, Turner could then feed information to the robbers about high-value loads and where they were going. Croke also invented a simple device to help with the robberies. He fashioned a device made up of a small box, fitted with a firing-pin, all attached to a belt. Inside the box was a 12-gauge shotgun shell. He would strap this device around a security guard's waist and show him a small remote control, which Dave claimed would work the firing-pin and explode the shotgun shell, blowing the guard's spine out. A truly terrifying innovation that would have any security guard ready to co-operate.

There was only one small problem. Dave knew that his device would never actually work; it was just a box, a shell and a moody remote with a red light on it. It was all smoke and mirrors. The only thing was that the guard would not know that it wouldn't work. Dave decided to try it out for the first time on a robbery he had been planning for a while.

Dave Croke had been following a security van for some months and knew there was over a million pounds in the back. He noted that the first stop of the day for the guards was at a warehouse called The Imperial Hops

Store, in Tottenham, north London, where one of the guards went inside and usually brought out a tray of tea and biscuits for the other two guards in the van. On the morning of the robbery, Dave Croke and Don Barrett, along with a third man, Croke's son-in-law, Glen, went to the Tottenham warehouse masked and armed. They quickly overpowered three workers and handcuffed them to a pipe. They then waited for the security van.

The van arrived just after 8am and, sure enough, one guard came in for the tea and was grabbed by the two robbers. Barrett held the guard at gunpoint while Dave showed him the device and explained in gory detail what would happen if he didn't co-operate. The belt was strapped around the waist of the guard and he was walked back to the van. The guard begged his mates inside the van to start throwing the money boxes out, he was crying real tears of fear. As the robbery was in progress, the manager of the premises arrived in his car and then tried to raise the alarm. The robbers fired at least two warning shots and subdued the manager. The guards in the back of the van eventually threw out three cash boxes and the robbers escaped with just over £90,000.

Dave was pleased that his device had the desired effect but he wanted more, and he knew how to get it. He embarked on a year-long plan to raid the Armaguard depot in Essex, where the money was loaded onto the vans. In the meantime, his son-in-law was passing back some very useful information from his job at the Shield Security depot at Nine Elms, Battersea. He had found out that every month there was a van heading up to Liverpool containing precious metals – gold, silver, platinum – and the plan was to rob it.

Just over a year after the Tottenham robbery, Dave Croke and Don Barrett followed the manager of the Essex Armaguard depot home. Masked and armed, they kidnapped the family – the manager, his wife and thirty-year-old daughter. The family were tied up and gagged. The robbers waited in the house until morning, when they untied the manager and strapped the belt with the device around his waist. He was driven to the depot by Croke, while Barrett waited at the manager's house, guarding the wife and daughter. The manager was instructed to open the vault, which he did. The robbers escaped with over £250,000 in cash. It was the biggest ever cash robbery carried out in Essex.

Unfortunately for David Croke, it was after this robbery that the police first got an inkling as to who they were after. It was Barrett's job to get rid of any incriminating evidence after the depot job but, instead of burning everything, he decided to dump it all in a dustbin two streets away from where Dave lived. The next day, a twelve-year-old boy saw a couple of latex old-man masks hanging from a bin and decided to delve deeper. He also found a leather belt in the bin with a small box attached to it and a remote control. He took the stuff home and showed his dad, who had only just watched the news describing the depot robbery and how the robbers were wearing old-man masks. The police were informed *tout de suite.*

Forensic evidence was gathered from the carelessly

discarded items and the name Don 'Crazy Horse' Barrett popped into the frame. The Flying Squad put Barrett under surveillance and noted him visiting Dave Croke's home. They also noted an Audi registered to George Ince parked outside Croke's house. The police kept close watch on the men and followed them for months. They knew they were dealing with seriously dangerous criminals who carried loaded firearms and were not afraid to fire off shots if things went King Kong, so this gang became a number-one priority for the Flying Squad. In the meantime, the gang were making plans to rob the precious-metals cargo from Shield Security.

The plan for the robbery was a simple one. Rita Croke's son, Alan, was on duty in the main depot at Battersea and would be privy to the top-secret information about cash and precious-metal movements. When he found out that there would be a large cargo of gold bars, gold coins, platinum and cash leaving the depot for Liverpool, he used a concealed phone to inform his father-in-law. Croke and Barrett plotted up across the road from the depot and picked up the van when it came out through the main gates. The robbers had all the information they would need: the registration number of the van, what it was carrying, how many guards (two) and, most important of all, which service station they stopped at on the journey for refuelling.

What the robbers did not know was that the police were on to them. The Flying Squad thought that the robbers plan was to raid the actual Shield Security depot, so they had eighty undercover police officers, as well as members of the police tactical firearms squad, PT17, focused on the depot. It turned out that Dave Croke did have a plan to empty the whole depot, but he was saving that for a future date. This robbery was about the £283,000 of gold bullion in the back of his son-in-law's armoured van.

The van left the Battersea depot, followed by the robbers in a blue Escort van. The police had set in for a long surveillance on the depot and had taken up OPs around the site, so only a handful were mobile and able to follow the convoy. The Shield Security van made its way through London and out on to the M1 motorway. The police were in disarray, passing urgent radio messages to their own men, having to get permission by radio to carry their firearms into another force's territory, and not knowing exactly where or how the robbers were going to make their move.

At Newport Pagnell service station, the Shield Security van pulled off the motorway, followed by the robbers' blue Escort, and the police in several unmarked vehicles. The police covertly watched as Alan Turner, who had been driving the security van, exited the vehicle and headed into the services. Inside he met up with Croke and Barrett, both dressed in suits, ties, surgical gloves and wigs. The robbers followed Turner back to the security van and quickly overpowered the other guard. Both guards were plasti-cuffed and bundled into the back of the van. Dave Croke climbed into the driver's seat and headed for the M1, with Barrett tailing him up in the blue Escort. The police were not close enough to clearly see what was going on, as they had parked in various secluded spots around the car park. But they had several marked pursuit vehicles parked on the hard shoulder of the M1 outside the services.

The Flying Squad officers saw that the Shield Security van was being driven by Croke as it headed towards the slip-road onto the motorway. The police order to 'Attack! Attack!' came over the airwaves, and the two vans were brought to an abrupt halt by police cars swerving in front and behind of them. Dave Croke was dragged from the security van and, after a brief struggle, was arrested. Barrett, surrounded by armed officers, stuck his hands in the air. When Croke was searched, he was found to have a loaded Colt .38 revolver in one pocket and a flick-knife and a cannister of CS gas in the other.

The only words spoken by Dave Croke at the time of his arrest and throughout his three-day detention in the police station were, 'I want my solicitor.' Don Barrett, on the other hand, was true to his nature. It was decided that, because of Barrett's previous attempt to become a supergrass, it might be worth confronting him and offering him a second chance to spill his guts. Barrett was arrested and, when he was confronted with the evidence, he caved in like a black hole. He gave up Dave Croke, he gave up the Tottenham robbery, the firearms supplier, the Armaguard robbery, along with several other security-van robberies they had committed. And he gave up Dave's son-in-law, who was driving the security van.

In the face of overwhelming evidence and the threat of his former compatriot coughing his lot in front of a jury, Dave Croke pleaded guilty to several counts of armed robbery and possession of firearms and explosives. He was sentenced to twenty-three years' imprisonment. Rita Croke's son, Alan Turner, was sentenced to seven years' imprisonment. Dave Croke's son-in-law, Glen, was sentenced to fifteen years' imprisonment. Croke's wife, Rita, was sentenced to eighteen months' imprisonment, suspended for two years. And Barrett? Barrett talked so much and so fast they thought he'd never shut up. He admitted twenty-three serious offences and was sentenced to sixteen years' imprisonment. This was reduced to twelve years and Barrett ended up serving a small fraction of that sentence in a comfortable supergrass suite. So, almost three decades after his first attempt, Don Barrett finally got his wish.

At this time, there had been 170 supergrasses in this country. The fact that years after Bertie Smalls had done the unthinkable, there were still major armed robbers willing and able to betray their former friends shows the state of the collective armed-robbery psyche at this time. Bertie Smalls had planted a poison seed in the minds of some criminals; a snaky get-out clause that would allow them to rob and pillage and then roll over and play spaniel when the time came to pay the price. And Bertie was still walking around London unharmed. A top police officer at the time of the Bertie Smalls deal had called him 'a craven, jackal of a man', and many in the criminal world have the same feelings for the supergrasses who were inspired by him, from Don Barrett to Stephen Roberts.

The parallels between the Wembley Mob of the

1960s and 1970s and the Dirty Dozen of the 1980s and 1990s are there for all to see. Both were professional bank-robbery gangs, targeting financial institutions in London; both were loose confederations of robbers who would work together and socialise together; both gangs managed to rob vast amounts of money; and both gangs were betrayed and brought down from within. The Dave Croke/Don Barrett case was in the news just around the time that the Bradish brothers and the rest of the Dirty Dozen were highly active in London. Stephen Roberts took a great interest in the case, perhaps making notes on how he might do a 'Bertie' or a 'Don' when the time came, as it inevitably would, for him to pay for his crimes.

As a footnote to the Dave Croke saga, after his release from prison for the Armaguard robbery, he was arrested in 1999 for murder, along with another well-known criminal, Bobby Knapp. They had apparently been hired by millionaire 'slumlord' Nicholas Van Hoogstraten to kill a business rival. In 2002, Van Hoogstraten was convicted of manslaughter and sentenced to ten years' imprisonment for the killing. The verdict was overturned on appeal and he was subsequently released but, in 2005, he was ordered to pay £6 million to the victim's family in a civil case.

Both Croke and Knapp were found guilty and sentenced to life imprisonment. David Croke hanged himself in his cell in Whitemoor top-security prison in November 2007. He was sixty-four.

Bertie Smalls died of natural causes in Croydon, south London, on 31 January 2008.

CHAPTER EIGHT

DRAGGING

One of the 'tools of the trade' employed by armed-robbery gangs is the motor vehicle. Almost from the beginning, law-breakers were using vehicles to commit or facilitate criminal acts. The police were not far behind in their use of motor vehicles to chase and harry the criminals. And so began a long game of cops and robbers that has lasted until the present day. There is no doubt that the motor vehicle has played its part in the prevalence of crime in the twentieth and twenty-first centuries, and was even the reason for the name 'Flying Squad', as they were the first police squad to use them.

For gangs like the Dirty Dozen, using cars and motorcycles was *de rigueur*; they needed to be able to cruise the streets while out looking for a target. The reason Stephen Roberts originally came to the attention of Sean Bradish was because of his reputed expertise as a car thief. A minority of young people in inner-city communities start their criminal careers by stealing cars and going for a joyride which usually means just driving about the area, showing off. The trouble is that this brings them easily to the attention of the police. Every joyrider will have stories of being chased by the police and there are some who steal cars and motorbikes just for the thrill of the chase.

Stephen Roberts started out as one of those young car thieves that stole cars just for the thrill of being able to drive around their own manor at the age of fifteen, but he pretty soon evolved into a good driver who loved nothing more than getting chased by several police cars, sirens blaring and lights flashing. He was arrested several times in his youth, and it was normally for what would be called 'petty nuisance offending' – car theft, theft of goods and property, and assault – but it would be this petty offending that brought him to the attention of the local ne'er-do-wells and villains.

One night in 1995, Sean Bradish was in the Coach & Horses having a drink after hitting a Thomas Cook shop earlier that day. He was flush with money and good humour, playing pool for fifty quid a game, drinking and snorting cocaine. He knew Roberts from occasionally seeing him around the manor. He knew he was mates with Steve Hall, who seemed like a pretty sensible geezer – at least, there were no dodgy whispers about him and that was a big plus in the tight-knit community of blaggers, draggers and carpet baggers of this corner of north-West London.

Sean was pretty pissed off that the car they had meant

to use for that day's robbery was an old rust-bucket Volkswagen Golf. The idea was to attract no attention to the getaway car, but he had pulled away from the job with thick black smoke coming from the exhaust. He may as well have been dressed in a clown's outfit and been waving a red flag. The trouble was that neither Sean nor anyone else in the gang was any good at stealing decent cars. The gang needed someone who could steal late-model cars that looked respectable, rather than old bangers that might get them a pull from the police before they had even reached the job. Sean challenged Roberts to a game of pool and got talking to him as they played. He decided that Roberts might be OK; he was known for his car-thieving skills and he was not an outsider. All Sean needed to do now was put Roberts to the test.

Sean had another robbery planned for the following week and he light a getaway car and a changeover car. The getaway car is driven to the scene of the robbery, the robbery is carried out and the getaway car is then driven to a pre-determined spot and abandoned. The changeover car will be parked close to the dumping spot, and the robbers decamp into it and carry on about their business. It is needed in case the getaway car is spotted at the job and reported to the police, who will then be on the lookout for that vehicle. Having a getaway and changeover vehicle is pretty standard for most professional armed-robbery gangs. You'd be mad not to use them. So Sean set Roberts the task of supplying two cars for this job.

Of course, Sean was no fool and had no intention of telling Roberts exactly what he needed these cars for. He assumed that Roberts could have a good guess, knowing that there were many rumours about what he and his little firm did for a living. But it is part of criminal etiquette that you ask no questions when you get involved in the outskirts of serious criminality. It is only when you have proved yourself and been fully accepted that you can then start to question. Roberts was delighted to be approached by Sean; he looked up to him and had long had a desire to be involved in getting some of the endless money that the gang seemed to have. He wanted the designer clothes, the BMWs and Audis that the gang drove around in, and the pretty girls who hung on every word that the members of this little firm uttered. For Roberts, this was like his dream was coming true.

Stealing certain makes and models of cars was as easy for him as putting his shoes on. He knew the security devices used by some car manufacturers and how to bypass them. Armed with his tools – a slide-hammer, large scissors and a centre-punch – he set out to fulfil Sean's order. The favourite getaway car of the original Dirty Dozen members was the Vauxhall Astra four-door, which was a perfect car for robberies. There were so many of them on the streets that, unless the car was bright pink or hot orange, it could blend in very nicely with other traffic. A getaway car didn't have to be supercharged or souped-up as there really was no great need for speed; it is more about anonymity than speed and power when it comes to getaway cars. The two things you want from a getaway car are that it works and that it doesn't stand out and attract attention.

Roberts checked out some of his favourite spots to steal

cars. Railway stations, car parks and quiet side streets. Railway stations were a favourite with a lot of car thieves because the odds are good that whoever has left their car there has gone off on a train and will not be close by if the alarm goes off. Roberts, like most car thieves, was not worried about car alarms – they would only be going off for a minute at the most before he disabled them – but it was only feasible if the actual owner of the car was not close by.

He was mooching around Wembley Station when he spotted the perfect target: a dark-blue VW Jetta estate, big enough for purpose and ordinary enough to blend in. He glanced around to make sure nobody was watching him and then walked confidently up to the car and jiggled the door lock with his scissors. After wrenching the scissors back and forth for a few seconds, he heard the satisfying click as the lock was forced open. He quickly opened the door and slipped into the driver's seat and got to work on the ignition lock with his handy slide hammer. The alarm was whooping but nobody even glanced in his direction; they were too busy going about their business to pay any attention to another alarm in a city of plenty. Less than three minutes after he had approached the car, he was pulling smoothly out of the car park.

Roberts parked the stolen VW on the Stonebridge estate in a spot where it was unlikely to be bothered and headed out to steal a second car. He found a nice dark-coloured four-door Astra in the car park of a Cricklewood supermarket and also parked this on the Stonebridge, but in a different spot. He phoned Sean on the number he had been given and told him the job had been done. Roberts was feeling pretty pleased with himself, as he believed he may have an 'in' into one of the most successful robbery teams in the country. By making himself useful to Sean, he was hoping he would now be able to get into at least one robbery with the gang. He was excited at the prospect but also a little fearful at what he might be getting into. The step from habitual, petty criminal to joining a successful armed-robbery gang was a massive one. For a start, getting caught stealing cars was not going to attract double-figure sentences in the same way armed robbery did. Roberts did not like prison and had no desire to languish there for a couple of decades. But he would cross that bridge when it presented itself.

Sean was happy with the cars that Roberts provided and used them on the planned robbery, which was successful and netted the gang almost £60,000. He felt magnanimous towards Robert after the robbery and slipped him £500 as a thank-you. He also suggested that, if Roberts was up for it, he could join them on the next job. Roberts was like a dog with two dicks.

CHAPTER NINE

EARLY DAYS: THE STREETS OF NORTH-WEST LONDON

Vincent 'Vinnie' Bradish interview with Andy Nolan

Vincent Bradish was born in Hillingdon Hospital, west London on 1 October 1963 to poor, working-class, Irish-immigrant parents. Their mother, a cleaner, was originally from Glin and their father, a factory worker, was from Foynes in County Limerick, close to the famous River Shannon. The family soon moved from Eastcote, west London to the densely Irish-populated area of Willesden in north-west London. Some of Vincent's early childhood memories were of the staff Christmas parties in the Wall's factory in Park Royal, where his father worked. Employees and their families were invited along. There were six brothers and three sisters in the typically large Irish Catholic Bradish brood. Ancestral research by the clan not surprisingly revealed a link to infamous pirates by the name of Bradish that had plagued the high seas in centuries past.

'God knows if we're related to them, but it wouldn't

feckin surprise me,' Vincent quips. 'Bradish and his crew were a rough bunch and they would loot all around them.'

Though anti-Irish sentiment was rife in the city during the late 1960s and early 1970s, neither Vincent nor his mother can recall any overt anti-Irish racism back then. However, it wasn't uncommon for the clan to be turfed out of several bed-and-breakfasts for no reason at a moment's notice, which, upon reflection, Vincent now finds strange. Recalling stories told to him by his mother, Vincent remarks that some landlords

wouldn't care less if they had nowhere else to stay; they'd throw them out for some minor reason and tell them to move on. We'd come back from somewhere and our bags would be packed, and we'd have to go. My mum's not loud or troublesome and my dad was working all the time. I'm sure they would've been paying their rent because she's an honest woman and he was just a normal, working guy. I can't see why they should've been kicking them out back in them days, the sixties and seventies. They'd just fling them out for any old reason, wouldn't they?

Vincent went to St. Joseph's Catholic primary school in Willesden. 'For me, I hated it,' he reflects. 'I hated it from the first time I went... I couldn't wait to get out at the end of every day. That's how it was, from the time I went to infant school to the time I left secondary school. I couldn't stand school. That's like a prison to me. Even when I drive past them nowadays and I see them with all the walls, and some of these schools have fences all around them – that's just like a prison to me and that's what it was like for me when I was a kid.'

Vincent was not involved in any street gang as a child and, as a teenager, he loved rock 'n' roll music.

We used to hang around with all the teddy boys and go into the club where they all hung out – The White Horse pub in Willesden. There used to be a club at the back of the pub called The Bobbysox Club and I used to go down there with my two younger brothers, Liam and Sean, and we'd go in there and dance away. The doorman would let us in most weeks, and we'd be dancing to the music, doing the bopping and jiving and everything. I was into the rock 'n' roll music when Elvis died – and the rockabilly music was great, and that's where I first came across 'Razor' [Noel 'Razor' Smith]. I didn't know him at the time, even though I'd seen him. I remember when I did meet him twenty years later and we started talking, I described the clothing that he used to wear. I goes, 'I can remember what clothes you used to wear when I seen you standing outside The Bobbysox Club.' He had a big angry head on him.

So how does a kid from a hard-working, law-abiding family become Scotland Yard's number-one target and the most prolific armed robber the UK has ever seen? The simple answer is poverty. At the age of fifteen, Vincent described himself as 'always stealing something because I had no money, so I'd be nicking things to get some money. If I couldn't afford something, I would nick it. Even as the years passed, I wasn't able to hold down a job. I knew Friday and Saturday were coming so I'd go around the shops nicking whatever I could – nicking a load of clothing and any bit of stuff and sell it so I could go out on a weekend.' At seventeen, Vincent was sent to a young offender's institution for theft, burglary and affray: 'I remember getting three months DC, which was the old Detention Centre where you were sent for what was known as the "Short, Sharp Shock". But I liked exercising anyway because I used to be in the army cadets when I was younger. I always liked running so it was easy enough for me, the DC. You were kept busy. They'd keep you on your toes from half five in the morning until you fell into your bed at night, knackered.'

The 'Short, Sharp Shock' was a policy introduced by the Conservative government in the early 1970s, by which juvenile offenders between the ages of fourteen and seventeen could be sentenced to either three or six months in a detention centre. The aim was to officially bully, brutalise and beat these young men into giving up their offending. The government wanted young offenders to be terrified of committing crime in case they were subjected to this punishment. It involved being beaten and assaulted by prison officers, being subject to 'boot camp'-style discipline and constant exercise, and having to having to do relentless work like scrubbing corridors with a toothbrush, breaking up cassettes with a toffee hammer or digging holes in a field and then filling them in. Some kids actually died from these regimes before they were scrapped in the early 1980s. The policy was never going to work because the one thing that the authorities seem to ignore when dealing with so-called deterrents is that no one goes out to commit a crime thinking they are going to be arrested; they think they are going to get away with it or they wouldn't do it. As an example of how ineffective deterrents are to criminals, you only have to look at the days when they used to publicly hang six or seven pickpockets at a time; crowds would gather to watch the spectacle of the executions – and pickpockets would work that crowd. If the sight of your confederates dangling on a rope was not enough to deter, nothing would be.

Asked how his wayward lifestyle was affecting his family, Vincent reflected: 'I suppose my family were sad, but my mum and dad thought, "It will probably liven him up," but it didn't really wake me up at all. Obviously, they would have preferred that I'd given it up. I done DC, Borstal and then prison. You couldn't go to prison until you were twenty-one. When I'd just turned twenty-one, I went to Camp Hill Prison[2] on the Isle of Wight for affray, malicious wounding and ABH.

2 HMP Camp Hill on the Isle of Wight was a Category C training prison, which took mainly young men from London and the surrounding areas. It was a very violent prison and known for its prisoner-on-prisoner violence. It was not unknown in Camp Hill for gang fights to break out in the exercise yard, sometimes involving up to twenty prisoners battering each other with makeshift clubs and other weapons. Camp Hill had a terrible reputation among young prisoners and was not the favoured destination for any prisoner from the mainland. Young men held in other prisons had been known to attempt suicide rather than be shipped to HMP Camp Hill. The prison was closed down for good in 2002.

'When I done Borstal, that was for burglaries, and DC was for theft and some other stuff. Nearly every year I was getting remanded for three or four months – when I was seventeen and eighteen – and that was until I met my girlfriend, my son's mum. When I met her, I quietened down a bit. I didn't get arrested for a good while you know.'

When asked if his family were fully aware of what he was doing, Vincent acknowledged, 'Yeah, of course, because it had been going on for years. To be hiding it and making out that you weren't doing it, you were taking everyone for a fool. By this time, I'd be working with the likes of Steven Roberts and a few others. Sometimes my mum would say to us, "You'd want to stay away from that fella, that Roberts. Stay away from him, he looks like no good." I'd say my ma was a very good judge of character in the end.'

Asked when he made the conscious decision that he wanted to be a career criminal, Vincent remarks: 'It just happened. I didn't make a conscious decision that I was gonna become a career criminal – I just turned into one. Almost by osmosis. Especially as I got older and I started committing the serious crime, like the armed robberies – that's what I would class as the career-criminal stuff because, before that, it was just petty stuff, in and out of work. If I wasn't working, I would nick whatever I could to make some money in between, but I was still working here and there doing whatever job I could get.'

It was around 1990 when, along with his younger brother, Sean, Vincent embarked on armed robbery.

Asked what it was like to cross the pavement and do a big robbery for the first time, Vincent recalled:

I remember thinking to myself, 'Fuck me, I wonder if I'll be able to speak if I have to speak in there,' you know. 'When I start demanding money, is the voice gonna come out?' We were wondering all this kind of stuff. You get the money and you run off up the road and you say 'fucking hell' – you can't believe it. Over in an instant. Nothing went into slow motion or nothing. I'd come out of the bank about ten grand richer after about ten or fifteen seconds. It was great.

Banks, building societies, security vans, bingo halls, cash in transit where they're picking up from bingo halls or from a supermarket – we would just attack them anywhere. Sometimes it would just be two of us, sometimes three. Sometimes we'd do a Thomas Cook.

We'd have done our scouting. Before we decided to rob the place, we drove around that area for weeks, or we might have driven there for a few months, and, as you were driving past places that we were thinking of robbing, we'd look at it quickly because we knew that the Old Bill would probably be following us. We always suspected that they were following us everywhere because we'd see them all the time. But the thing is they never knew when we were gonna attack the premises, so we would drive over this way, drive that way and be looking at escape routes, and we'd talk about them later.

The Thomas Cooks, sometimes we'd go in there and you could get fifty or a hundred grand, a load of traveller's cheques and a load of foreign currency. They were good for us.

That was back in the days when you were going out clubbing it to raves and all that stuff. You'd be dancing away in the club and you'd be thinking of the robbery during the morning... and you're just buzzing. Yeah it was brilliant and, when people used to start talking about normal work – building work – I would just think to myself, 'Why talk about that crap? That's just crap. If you knew what I had just done today.' It really makes you start thinking, 'What a waste of time.' A person working all day from eight till five to get a few quid when you can go into a bank and get twenty grand in less than thirty seconds and just disappear into thin air. By time you get into your car, the Old Bill are just getting a call and you're off up the road with twenty or thirty grand. It was just too easy. They're heading to the bank and you're driving home. They don't even know what you look like. They're all going the wrong way.

We'd be in the car laughing and thinking, 'What a bunch of fucking eejits. They're chasing the wrong guys.' We'd just be laughing our heads off, driving up the road about thirty or forty grand richer, you know. It's just ridiculous. Why are they calling them the Flying Squad when they can't catch anyone? I was never arrested doing a robbery. I've never been arrested with a firearm. It was good fun while it lasted.

Wearing balaclavas and surgical gloves, one of the brothers – normally Sean – would hold a sawn-off shotgun to a victim and demand money, threatening to blow their head off. Any onlookers would be threatened with being taken hostage.

Some jobs were planned out quite meticulously and some were done on the spot. If we knew the Old Bill were following us but we needed some money, we'd still commit a robbery. We would just do some mad anti-surveillance techniques, driving around roundabouts three or four times, going up one-way streets, indicate right and then go left and then you would do a spur-of-the-moment thing. A security van went past one day and we just parked up the motorbikes, jumped off, ran into the bank after him, and I really wasn't in the mood because I'd been out the night before on the piss, so I had a bit of a sore head that morning. I just told him, 'Open up the box, you fucking eejit,' or something like that. 'Open it, come on, lively,' and he opened it up straight away. Threw a bag of cash at me – twenty-five grand. And that was about the quickest bit of work that I ever done. That took about ten seconds. Me, Roberts and Sean were convicted of that robbery. That could happen quite a bit.

Sometimes we would be driving around looking for something, just looking for a security guard and, if he's in the right place and we can catch him in between the bank and the van, we'd have him. You're watching everything and everyone. If I see a dodgy look out of one geezer, or he looks the wrong way and I get the vibe from him that he's the Old Bill, you ain't got no time for jokes. But we didn't beat anyone up or shoot anyone on a robbery. We weren't interested in that. All we were interested in is getting the money and going as quick as possible. And that was that.

Along with its huge Irish community, the north-west corner of London that the Bradish boys operated in was also home to a very large Afro-Caribbean community, particularly around Harlesden, Stonebridge and Ladbroke Grove. Asked if there was any friction between the white and black criminal gangs, Vincent recalled:

There was no friction or rivalry. Nearly everyone from around Harlesden knew what we was at because we were going around in nice, fancy motors – BMW convertibles – we were flying around on motorbikes – 600cc – and, by the look of it, not doing a stroke of legitimate work, and it was going on for years. Everyone knew what we was at, but they wouldn't know exactly what you'd done. You wouldn't tell no one what you'd done; they just knew what you'd done and that's it – there'd be nothing to speak about. Even when you went to the pub, you wouldn't be speaking about it because there's nothing to speak about. It's like when you go to work all day, you don't go to the pub and start talking about your job in the evening because you're sick to fecking death of it, but we weren't sick to death of our job – you just wouldn't speak about it. But in regards to the Afro-Caribbean gangs, you'd meet them down at the pub and they never bothered us, we never bothered them. We know a lot of black people from around Brent. That's where we were brought up. There was no friction at all; everyone got on fine. We used to drink in a club where we would be the only five or six white men playing dominoes and smoking with about one hundred black people.

Vincent went on to declare:

We wouldn't mix with celebrities. When we were doing our stuff, we would just stay in our own area. Even if we made ten grand that day, or thirty or fifty grand, we'd stay around Harlesden or Stonebridge, drinking in our local pubs. We wouldn't go up to the West End – we wouldn't bother. We spent all our money back around Harlesden. We were happy drinking in our local pub, having a few pints of Guinness. Everything that we robbed we put back into the community. If the money was ruined with red dye, we would just drive through the high street, throwing it all out the windows of the car. People would be picking it up and spending it in the pubs and clubs around Harlesden. That way, if ever we got caught with money with red dye on it, we had the perfect alibi: 'Yeah, it was flying all around Harlesden. Everyone's got it. What's the crime?'

Mixing with the Afro-Caribbean population rubbed off on Vincent in particular: 'When I was growing up, I listened to reggae music all the time – smoking the weed every week and that became every day. We grew up with all that. As well as the rock 'n' roll, reggae was the music we loved.'

I well remember first meeting Vinnie Bradish back in the 1980s – he was a regular at The Bobbysox Club. A bit younger than me, but noticeable for their gameness, both the Bradish brothers stood out from the rest. I had already served a three-year prison sentence for armed robbery and, though the Bradish boys were not really serious criminals at this stage, I could sense that they were more than capable. When I was working with a robbery team in the 1990s, known as The Laughing Bank Robbers, we would raid banking premises in north-west London in order to divert attention from where we lived in south London, but little did we know that the Bradish brothers had the same idea and would come over from north-west London in order to raid targets in our area of south London. Our two separate robbery teams would even target the same premises. It was like we were inexplicably linked. Particularly so when we all ended up in Whitemoor prison together serving massive prison sentences . . .

CHAPTER TEN

ROBERTS: THE EARLY YEARS

'I was making a living from robbing drug dealers,
something I'd started with a couple of old school friends a
few years earlier. We had become quite sophisticated. [...]
It was a good living. One time we came away with £46,000
in cash, another time we got a kilo of cocaine. The best
thing about it was that, no matter what we did, no matter
how much violence we used, it was the perfect crime
because they couldn't go to the police.'

Steven Roberts

The crack house looked exactly like what it was: a
dirty, run-down council flat on a south-London estate.
It was a ground-floor flat, the path to the door littered
with broken plastic crack vials and shiny, silver, torpedo-
shaped nitrous-oxide containers glittering slightly in
the weak late autumn sun. Steven Roberts and his two
friends, Chris and Roy, watched the front door from the
balcony of an adjacent block, two floors up.

111

They had decided that it would be safer to carry out this bit of work well away from their own north-west-London manor. Less chance of being recognised. They had found out about the target from a friend of Roy's, who used the place to score on a regular basis. He had told them that it was run by a Yardie (ie. Jamaican, because many Jamaicans called their home their 'yard', hence the gang name 'Yardies'), wannabe who went by the handle of 'Shimmers'. A dangerous scrote, by all accounts, but not really connected to any of the big crews in the drug world. As far as Roberts and his little firm were concerned, it was a liberty just waiting to be taken.

Roberts was the brains of the outfit, although that wasn't saying much. The three had known each other since secondary school, smoked their first spliff together and set out on their lives of crime as teenage confederates. First a bit of petty theft, shoplifting and stealing from motor vehicles. Then they moved on to car theft, mainly for joyriding and posing for the local girls while pulling handbrake turns in stolen Cortinas and Volkswagen Golfs. Next they got into burgling local flats and houses, which gave them the wherewithal to invest in a parcel of hashish to deal to their mates.

Roberts and his little firm had no love of work and a contempt for the people who were too stupid to see the light. Their lives of leisure suited them: wake up around 10am, first spliff of the day, stumble out of bed and wait for the day to develop – it was a great life. They were earning a nice little wedge from selling hash and had lately been getting involved in dealing small amounts of cocaine and heroin, which meant they were rarely short of money. But Roberts began to get restless. Deep in his heart, he just knew that he should be enjoying the best of everything and he believed he was destined for greater things. Chris and Roy had come up with the idea to start robbing drug dealers when they had seen the amount of cash and drugs involved. It was almost the perfect crime because there was no way that their victims could even report it to the police. What were they going to say? 'Hey, Mr Officer, they stole my drugs'?

It was the Jamaican gangs, or Yardies, who made a criminal business out of robbing drug dealers and suppliers. They called it 'taxing', as in taking their tax from the dealers. On the whole, most Yardie gangsters would deal out over-the-top violence while committing their crimes. It was nothing to them to shoot up a crack-den with a sub-machine gun in order to get what they wanted. Their motto was 'It's a good life, but a short life' and they held life very cheaply indeed.

An example of the crazy violence of the Yardie gangs and their propensity to use firearms is illustrated by two prisoners who shared a landing-spur with both me and Vinnie Bradish at HMP Whitemoor in Cambridgeshire. Known by the unlikely nicknames of 'Run Tings' and 'Scare Dem', they were part of a Yardie gang known as The Lock City Crew, who murdered innocent bystander Dion Holmes in late 1999. The two were called, along with other members of their posse, to the Bridge Leisure Centre in Wembley after a member of a rival posse insulted one of their wives in a row over parking. Yes, parking!

The Lock City Crew brought a holdall full of guns and locked the doors in the leisure centre so that nobody could get out. They then proceeded to fire off shots from several firearms, including a pump-action shotgun, a machine-pistol and automatic handguns. Looking at the evidence photos, with each shell-case marked and numbered by police-evidence officers, is enough to see that this gang were firing fast, often and indiscriminately. When it comes to life-ending violence, the Yardies have got it covered.

This is why robbing crack-houses, which were often run by or guarded by Yardies, was a very dangerous business. But Roberts and his firm had armed themselves and were hoping to include the element of surprise in their attack. Chris and Roy had already tried a move on a local drug dealer but getting into the premises had proved tricky. The trouble was that both men looked like exactly what they were – criminals. It was decided that a white face and a better plan was needed.

Up on the balcony, the three would-be robbers watched as a Mercedes sports car rolled onto the estate, bass-heavy drum and bass music pounding from the interior. The car stopped and two men got out, both black and in their early thirties, smartly dressed in casual but expensive clothes and trainers, and with the occasional flash of bling from neck, wrist, fingers and teeth in the weak sunlight. Roberts and his firm watched as the two new arrivals, one carrying a small sportsbag, walked up to the flat and hammered loudly on the front door. The door was opened and the two men disappeared inside.

Robert, Chris and Roy began to walk quickly down the

staircase to the ground-floor flat. 'That was Shimmers. He owns five crack-dens in this area,' said Chris as they approached the flat. Roy nodded vigorously.

Roberts swallowed hard and said, 'Let's hope they're not tooled up.'

The three men walked out of the estate to where a Volkswagen Golf GTI was parked. They got into the car, Roberts in the driving seat. He twisted a screwdriver that was hanging from the ignition and the car roared into life. Roberts had stolen the VW himself from a supermarket car park in Cricklewood the night before. They drove back onto the estate and parked out of sight of the crack-den.

The three men exited the car, with Roberts walking straight up the short path to the front door, and Chris and Roy slipping off to each side so that they couldn't be seen from the door. Roberts reached into his pocket and pulled out a couple of £20 notes. He held them in his hand ready for the show. He nodded to his two companions and then banged loudly on the door. After a couple of seconds, he saw a chink of light behind the door as someone snicked the spyhole cover open and observed him.

'What you want?' The voice from inside the crack-den was deep and muffled.

'I need something, bruv,' Roberts said, using the wheedling inflection in his voice used by a lot of clucking junkies.

'Ya 'ave money?' The voice sounded hopeful.

'I got paper, bruv!' Roberts waved the two £20 notes in front of the spyhole.

There followed the sound of locks and bolts being undone behind the door, which then swung open to reveal a fat, light-skinned black man, aged about twenty-five. He was wearing a dirty-looking yellow vest and blue Adidas tracksuit bottoms, along with a pair of dirty white trainers. The vest had so many food stains on it that, if you had boiled it, you could probably have got a nourishing soup out of the leftover water. His moon-like face looked clammy and unhealthy, his dark eyes sunken and half-closed.

Roberts stepped forward and whipped a wicked-looking 18-inch machete from inside his jacket. He swung the Sheffield steel towards the face of the fat doorman but missed by a hair's breadth as the would-be victim threw himself backwards in fear. Chris and Roy, both also waving large machetes, piled into the flat, shouting and screaming like banshees. Chris grabbed the fat doorman by his short dreadlocks and launched him into the front room. They burst in on 'Shimmers' and a couple of others with a quarter of a kilo of cocaine unwrapped on a small coffee table. Bingo!

Roberts swung his machete and caught one of the men on the forehead. Immediately, blood gushed from the wound and splashed the coffee table and the unwrapped cocaine. Chris had 'Shimmers' by the throat, holding him against a wall, with the point of his razor-edged machete under his left eye. 'I tek ya bloodclaat eye clean out, you likkle pussy'ole,' he hissed into the dealer's shocked face. Roberts stood in the middle of the small room, holding his machete at arm's length, pointing it slowly from one man to another.

'Don't get killed over a bit of food,' he shouted. 'Now everybody get on the floor!'

When the victims were on the floor, Roy found a plastic carrier bag in a kitchen drawer and began to load the drugs into it. Chris was stripping everyone in the place of any cash or jewellery they might have, and Roberts stood with his weapon raised threateningly. They moved fast, fearful that their entry may have attracted unwanted attention. Within a few minutes of entering the building, they were on their way out with the prize. They swiftly made their way to the stolen Golf GTI and wheel-spun off the estate with a squeal of rubber and a roar of engines on their way back to Kilburn.

The robbery on the south-London crack-house had netted a quarter of a kilo of almost pure cocaine and a bit of gold, a fake Rolex watch and £600 in cash. And this success assured them that they were onto a winner – robbing drug dealers was the future for this little firm.

The details of the above robbery were given to me by a friend of Roberts' who wishes to remain anonymous for various reasons, not least being that he was involved in the robberies. He also told me that Roberts' statement to the police about how he committed drug-firm robberies was just another figment of Roberts' overactive imagination. For the purposes of this book, I will call him 'Ernie'.

I met up with Ernie in a greasy-spoon café in Kilburn on a cold October morning. Dressed head to toe in designer leisurewear and sporting at least three gold teeth, he told me that he was now a drug dealer himself. Though he intimated that he was one of the big boys in the game, I suspected he was a bit lower on the ladder than he was making out, particularly judging by the rusting and smoking Ford he turned up in. Over sausage sandwiches and strong tea, I asked him to tell me what he knows about Steven Roberts days of robbing drug dealers.

'Yeah, we did rob plenty of people in those days – it was the game man. Steve was up for it, we all were, it was easy money. The people we was robbing couldn't go to Old Bill so they just had to take a back seat and swallow.'

I asked him about Roberts statement about going to rob crack-houses dressed as a police officer. He laughed, long and loud.

'Boy! That would be the most stupid fucking idea ever, man. Think about it, you're running a crack-den, so the last person you are going to let into your premises is a white man waving a police badge and asking to "use the phone"! What fucking phone? Seriously...'

I asked why he thought that Roberts had made such a statement to the police?

'The guy was just saying anything that sounded good to them. From what I've heard, most of his statements were bullshit; he was telling them what they wanted to hear. That's the fucking game, man, and Steve was good at the game. Don't get me wrong, we robbed plenty of drug dealers, he wasn't lying about that. And he wasn't lying about the violence either. Sometimes we had to torture men to get them to give the food and that. But not dressed like Old Bill, man, that's just nonsense.'

CHAPTER ELEVEN

AT IT

According to British law, Section 8 (1) of the Theft Act 1968, the act of robbery is defined thus: *A person is guilty of robbery if he steals, and immediately before or at the time of doing so, and in order to do so, he uses force on any person or puts or seeks to put any person in fear of being then and there subjected to force.*

So, to cut a long story short, robbery is stealing with threats of violence. It is a dangerous crime, not only for the victims but also for the perpetrators. British police have had a tendency to shoot first and ask questions long after when confronted by armed men. Many armed robbers, particularly in London, believe that in the 1980s and 1990s Special Operations 8 (commonly known as the Flying Squad) had a 'shoot to kill' policy against armed robbers in the capital.

Some people may have the tendency to view the crime of professional armed robbery as a bit of a caper. The kind of crime that does not really impinge on the lives of ordinary people and only affects banking institutions and cash-in-transit companies, and, on the whole, they are half-right. Yes, the robbing of cash or valuables at the point of a gun is a problem for the companies who lose out financially, but sometimes ordinary people are caught up in the commission of a robbery and these are the ones who are most traumatised. It can be no fun going about your daily business, as an ordinary member of the public, only to suddenly be confronted by masked gunmen. The emotional and mental fallout from just being in close proximity to an armed robbery can be vast.

Of course, this is mainly the fault of the men with the masks and guns who choose to threaten and rob for a living, rather than going to work like upright members of the public. Also, it does not help that some banking institutions have a policy that only allows their staff to hand over the cash if their customers are directly threatened. This information has been known for at least a couple of decades and would-be robbers know that, in order to claim the prize, sometimes they will have to directly threaten bank customers with their weapons.

The Dirty Dozen knew the game, as anyone taking up such a serious and dangerous occupation should, and they acted accordingly. Putting loaded (or even unloaded) guns at the heads of innocent customers is anathema to most people but, if your job is robbing others of their money, you tend to depersonalise your victims in order to give yourself permission to carry out the crime. The truth is that the majority of professional robbers are not out to kill or maim; they want the money and accept that they may have to do ruthless and horrible things in order to get it. Unlike other violent criminals, such as murderers, GBH merchants or football hooligans, violence – or, more likely, the threat of violence – is instrumental to the crime. The perfect armed robbery, from the perpetrators point of view, would be to get the prize and get clean away with nobody physically hurt. Hurting or shooting people on armed robberies only gets the police and the public spotlight shining on you, and adds more years to the already stiff sentence you will get if convicted of the crime. And no criminal worth his salt would want that.

Thursday, 8 June 2000

Sean and Vinnie Bradish met up with Stephen Roberts on a bright summer morning in the Willesden area of north-west London. Money was running low and it was time to get on the rob again. Vinnie was riding a blue Suzuki, while Roberts was riding pillion on Sean's black Honda CBR 600. They cruised the streets with their eyes open for a prize – any prize that looked like it could be taken. At first, they rode in convoy but, after a while, Vinnie peeled off to run his eye over a Securicor delivery at a supermarket. It was a no-go, as there was a police patrol car parked further down the road. At this stage, none of the gang was that worried about being nicked by uniformed plod – after all, they had enough firepower wrapped around them to threaten or shoot their way out of most situations – but they could do without pulling one off right under the noses of the local *gendarmes*. A shootout on Willesden High Street on a summer's morning was nothing but a spotlight pointing towards their activities.

While Vinnie was checking on the supermarket, Sean and Roberts spotted a blue Securicor van in the grounds of Willesden Hospital. Sean glanced at his watch. It was 11.15am. For the professional robber, checking the time when a van is spotted at a stop is always good information to have as, even if it didn't become a target on the spot, you would know where and what time it stopped for a future robbery. One of the most essential tools for serious crime is information, and most professional criminals will collect it and file it away at every opportunity. It becomes natural for the criminal to be hyper-vigilant and to hold vast amounts of possibly helpful information in his head.

Sean slowed the Honda and Roberts jumped off the pillion. This was part of their well-rehearsed routine. No words needed to be spoken; both men knew the steps of this familiar dance very well. Roberts walked into the grounds of the hospital and watched the van from a distance while giving the impression that he might be waiting for a friend. Which he was.

Sean gunned the powerful Honda around the backstreets to where he had a black duffel-bag stashed in the boot of a parked car. Sean pulled up behind the old Vauxhall and quickly flipped the boot-lid before grabbing the bag and jumping back onto his bike. Within three minutes he was riding through the entrance to the hospital. Sean parked the Honda up and was joined by Roberts. They stashed the crash helmets with the bike, and both put bandannas across the lower part of their faces and wore baseball caps pulled low. They were about 600 feet from the van but hidden from view by bushes. Sean reached into the duffel-bag and pulled out a double-barrelled, sawn-off, 12-bore shotgun. He clicked the fearsome-looking weapon open and Roberts could see the two brass striking plates of the cartridges. Sean snapped the gun shut with a satisfying metallic thwack and nodded. 'Let's fucking have it,' he snarled and began to walk towards the van and the so-far unsuspecting guards.

As the robbers approached the van, a uniformed security guard was coming out of the entrance to the hospital. There were a couple of nurses and patients smoking just outside the entrance and it was quite a tranquil summer scene. Until Sean Bradish and Stephen Roberts suddenly appeared in the midst of it all like a couple of Tasmanian devils, screaming orders and obscenities at the tops of their gruff cockney voices. One minute there was relative silence, just the quiet hum of conversation and the chirping of birds, and then it was a maelstrom of movement and terrifying noise.

Sean ran to the guard and grabbed him by the collar of his shirt. He slammed him into the side of the van, poked the sawn-off into his face and told him to open the box he was carrying or Sean would 'blow his fucking head off!' Roberts watched the smokers outside the entrance. Their mouths seemed to fall open in unison as they watched this drama being played out in front of their eyes. Roberts pulled a large wrench from inside his jacket and feinted a run towards the innocent smokers, letting them know that, if they got involved in something that wasn't their business, there would certainly be a painful price to pay. Seeing the smokers were shocked, subdued and unlikely to cause a problem, Roberts then hammered the wrench on the side of the security van and shouted for the guard inside to start throwing the cash out.

There is always a risk when robbing security vans on spec that the guard may have already delivered the cash, or that they will try to fob you off with a dummy box, and, as time is of the essence in these cases – the average robbery being no more than three long minutes –the robbers must know when to cut their losses and vacate the premises.

In this case, things turned sour pretty quickly. The guard inside the van decided to follow company policy: no matter how much danger the outside guard was in, no large amounts of cash were to be handed over. Truly a company for which cash is much more important than the safety of its employees. For a moment, no money was forthcoming, so Sean put the barrels of his gun under the chin of the outside guard and looked into his terrified eyes, all the better to convey his violent intentions. The guard swallowed hard and managed a plaintive shout: 'Carol, give them the money. Don't fuck about – they're serious!'

The standard and unmerciful company answer came back like a slap in the face: 'I can't. It's in the safe.'

The outside guard knew that this wasn't true, but there was fuck all he could do about it except mentally curse

Carol's stubborn diligence. The outside guard let out a strangled and desperate wail. He had dropped the cash box he had been carrying and Roberts turned his attention to this. He slapped the guard on the side of his crash helmet. 'Open that fucking box,' he growled. But suddenly, also as company policy, Carol threw out two large bags of coins, which hit the road with two loud thumps.

Roberts left the guard and rushed to check what had come out of the van. Each bag contained around £2,000 in loose coins. The bags were too heavy to take on the bike and not worth the aggravation. Roberts, frustrated and angry, banged hard on the van. 'We'll fucking kill him, Carol, no joke!'

There was movement inside the van, then a grey Securicor cash bag dropped from the hatch. Roberts was on it like a dog on a tasty bone. He quickly ripped the bag open and discovered it was a dummy bag, full of brand-new paper cut into the shape of bank notes. Roberts turned on the guard, grabbing him away from Sean's grip and growling into his face, 'Open the box or I'll punch your fucking face in!' This seemed like a mild threat considering Sean had already had the gun in his face and threatened to blow his head off, but time was running out and so were ideas. With that, the alarm inside the van was activated and it was time to go.

Sean grabbed the Securicor box from the ground near the guard's feet and, with Roberts, he ran for the Honda. He passed the box to Roberts and started the bike, speeding out of the hospital grounds and off towards Harlesden.

Sean pulled into the Curzon Crescent estate, just off Drayton Road in W10. They jumped off the bike and attempted to smash open the Securicor cash box. They took turns in smashing the metal box against walls and the kerb, but with no luck. Then the alarm on the box began to sound, like an old-fashioned ambulance siren, and the red dye-pack inside exploded and emitted a stream of red marker smoke. The robbers could hear police sirens in the surrounding area and decided that they were never going to open the box before the police tracked it to their location. A lot of cash-in-transit boxes now used GPS trackers as well as other security devices, so it was vital for the robbers to distance themselves from the box as quickly as possible.

Realising that they were on a loser, Sean dumped the now smoking and wailing cashbox into a wheelie-bin and slammed the lid. They were up on the Honda and moving again before the police got too close. Sean rode towards his mother's house in nearby Bishops Way, intending to park the bike and change clothing. On route, Sean rode down an alleyway off St Thomas Street and dropped the sawn-off, now wrapped in a bin-liner, into a bin for later retrieval.

Sean parked the Honda around the back of his mum's place and he and Roberts went inside. According to Roberts' statement to the police on 15 January 2001, inside the house Sean immediately got a pair of clippers and cut his own hair in order to alter his appearance. Both men changed their clothing and Roberts borrowed a red jumper from Sean. Once they were changed, Sean got Vinnie on the phone and found out that he was at the flat of one of the hangers-on, John O'Callaghan. John lived in a flat above a launderette in Harlesden High Street and it was sometimes used to store guns, the robbery kit or for meetings.

Stephen Roberts said in court that, when he and Sean turned up at O'Callaghan's place and found Vinnie there, also present were other gang associates Danny Mac, wearing a white baseball cap and white shirt, and Stephen Wall. Roberts states: 'Tony Hall used to store a number of guns inside O'Callaghan's flat – either his own or Sean Bradish's. I've seen a single-barrelled shotgun, a double-barrelled side-by-side shotgun and a double-barrelled under-and-over shotgun. All were sawn-offs. These were kept in a blue sports bag in a cupboard. There came a time when O'Callaghan no longer wanted these in his flat and Tony Hall removed them and stored them in a locker at his health club, Cannings Health Club in Monks Park, behind a car-rental firm.'

After about an hour, when all the furore had died down and the sirens had faded, Sean told Vinnie where he had hidden the shotgun and asked him to pick it up. With John O'Callaghan riding pillion, Vinnie rode to the alley and waited as O'Callaghan retrieved the gun from the bin. The gun was to be kept in O'Callaghan's place until it was needed again. Sean and Roberts decided to take a walk around the area to see if they could spot any police activity.

According to Roberts, the reason for him committing this attempted robbery on spec was because his drug use was spiralling out of control and he was rinsing through cash at a rate of knots. His heroin and cocaine use had gone from occasional to every day as he stole more and more money with the gang. The others only suspected how much gear Roberts was consuming. His moods were up and down, and even Mrs Bradish, Sean and Vinnie's mother, remarked that he looked like a junkie and should not be trusted. And, as Vinnie was to remark some years later, 'My mother was on the ball about that fella. She knew he was no good.'

Sean had committed the attempted robbery on the security van simply because he was always up for it – it was his job as far, as he was concerned. And Vinnie was also always up for an adventure that would lead to a few more quid in his pocket. The thing that the general public have difficulty getting their heads around is crime as a full-time job, but most professional criminals accept it as the norm.

CHAPTER TWELVE

TOOLING UP

Armed robbery, by its very definition, requires the participants – certainly the robbers – to be armed with a weapon. Their choice of weapon and how they use it generally depends on the disposition of the robber and the availability of weapons. The Dirty Dozen had plenty of access to firearms, which were cheap and plentiful in London in the 1980s and 1990s. Servicemen returning from the Falklands War in the early 1980s brought with them many war souvenirs, including pistols that they had taken from Argentinian prisoners of war. The Argentinians favoured the Browning Hi-Power 9 mm, the M1911 Colt .45, the Sistema Colt Modelo 1927 (a copy of the Colt M1911, built under license in Argentina) and the Ballester-Molina .45. Colt and Browning handguns were already quite popular among UK criminals and were familiar, but the Ballester-Molina .45, which looks very like the Colt, began to show up for sale. As a seven-shot semi-automatic pistol, the Ballester-Molina soon became popular with Yardie gunmen and armed robbers alike.

Another favourite of the armed 1990s criminal was the Brocock air-cartridge pistol. Brococks – ostensibly air pistols – were imported and distributed by a Birmingham-based company. When used legally, the pistols fired .177 pellets using a compressed-air cartridge that is loaded into the gun and were pretty harmless and definitely non-lethal unless fired directly into the eye. But it soon became clear to criminal armourers with an interest in such market innovations that, by fitting these guns with steel sleeves inside the chamber, it would convert the pistol to live and allow it to fire a standard .22 bullet. In the hands of experts, the barrel could be further drilled out in order to allow the gun to fire a more lethal .38 round. By December 2002, the NCIS stated that Brocock pistols accounted for 35 per cent of all guns recovered by police. The Association of Chief Police Officers (ACPO) called for a 'national ban' on Brocock air pistols.

Though handguns of all types were available through backstreet armourers, a lot of armed robbers favoured the sawn-off shotgun. As a frightener, the sawn-off could not be beaten. With its shortened barrels, making for a wider spread of shot, the shotgun is a fearsome-looking weapon capable of inflicting great damage. Unlike assassins, hit-men or other brandishers of firearms, armed robbers are not generally looking to actually shoot anyone. As previously mentioned, their weapons have the sole purpose of instilling fear and co-operation and, for this, the sawn-off shotgun fits the bill perfectly. It is a little-known fact that actually sawing the barrels from a shotgun – i.e. shortening the barrels – is a criminal offence punishable by two years' imprisonment. According to the law, the only reason to shorten the barrels of a gun is for concealment, in order to commit an unlawful offence. If you are arrested with a full-length shotgun without a licence, the chances are fifty-fifty that you will end up in prison, depending on mitigation and circumstances. But a sawn-off shotgun is jail time straight off the bat and no mitigation or circumstances will be brooked.

Some amateur robbers foolishly think that, by using an unloaded gun or an imitation gun, they will be treated leniently by the courts if captured in the commission of an armed robbery, but this is definitely not the case. It is the threat that is paramount in proving a charge of robbery, so it doesn't matter if you are carrying a nickel-plated .357 Magnum revolver with hollow-point rounds, or a gun-shaped potato wrapped in a bag – if the victims fear for life and limb, you will be going to prison for a long stretch. So the majority of professional robbers have the attitude that they may as well be hung for a sheep as a lamb when it comes to going armed.

Professional robbers take themselves and their profession very seriously, and will usually have a real and live firearm while committing their crimes. The reasons for this are pretty obvious: if they find a stubborn security guard or a have-a-go-hero member of the public, it wouldn't be much use shouting 'Bang!' at them; sometimes the sound of a gun going off is needed to galvanise the action. Many robbers of my acquaintance are what are known as 'crash-bang' merchants: they use surprise and shock to their advantage, 'crashing' open the door of a bank and then 'banging' a shot into the ceiling in order to get everyone's attention. This would be a lot less effective using imitation firearms.

No armed robber goes out with the deliberate intention to shoot somebody during a robbery but, on rare occasions, things can get out of hand and it is better to have a gun and not need it than to need a gun and not have one. There is a certain amount of confidence in having a working and loaded firearm with you on a bit of work. And let's be realistic here: sometimes the only way to keep your liberty is by being prepared to give someone a lead injection, be it in the leg or anywhere else. We are talking about armed and desperate criminals, after all.

In the late 1980s, there was a spate of 'armed' robberies in London by various unusual characters using a variety of fake guns. One East End criminal named Ernie Covely robbed several building societies with a large cucumber in a paper bag, apparently eating the 'firearm' in sandwiches after the robbery. Inevitably, the tabloids nicknamed him 'Cucumber Man'. When he was caught and convicted, he was jailed for nine years. Likewise, a witless young robber from the Woolwich area used a banana for the same purpose and managed to get away with several thousand pounds before the prison gates slammed behind him. 'Banana Man', as he was nicknamed by the press, got ten years in prison for his fruit-related japes. He also disposed of his 'gun' by eating it. One enterprising robber hit several high-street banks with a fake bomb made from a box of cornflakes and some old wiring. He would place his bag on the counter with the wires from the cereal box sticking out, and then pass a note to the cashier telling her he had a bomb and he wanted money. Surprisingly, perhaps, this not-so-bright plan actually worked, and he managed to clear a few thousand pounds before the boom fell. Of course, he ended up in prison for seven years.

So, if you are going to prison for years for having something shaped like a firearm, you might as well carry a real one. This is the hard-earned message that the majority of armed criminals have now taken on board. The Bradish gang were not out-and-out killers – they did not want to kill anyone, or even to shoot anyone unless it was absolutely necessary to preserve their own lives and liberty – so guns were just tools of the trade to them. None of them had a real favourite gun, although Sean seemed to favour the Magnum revolver, and would use whatever gun was available at the time.

CHAPTER THIRTEEN

'THE POLICE ARE ON US'

On Monday, 3 July 2000, the boys were once again on the hunt for a cash prize, this time around Greenford in Middlesex. Roberts was again riding pillion on Sean's motorbike. They were being tailed by Danny Mac in his red Honda motor car with black-tinted windows and shiny alloy wheels. The car was bound to attract attention, so Sean ordered him to keep well back. Danny was short of cash and had agreed to come along and keep a discrete watch on Sean's bike, as they would park it away from the site of the robbery. If the Bradish gang were hyper-vigilant when committing crimes, their one mistake was to use their own vehicles while out on spec. They usually used stolen cars or motorbikes as their getaway vehicles, but sometimes could not be bothered with the minutiae of stealing vehicles and would rely on parking their vehicles out of immediate sight of a robbery. Their thinking was that, if any of their own vehicles were compromised, it would not matter because none of them were registered as belonging to them, and money was so easy to come by that they would just buy new vehicles to replace the ones that had been compromised.

As Sean rode into Sudbury Hill, he spotted a Barclays that he had robbed before. It always makes me chuckle when people say that lightning doesn't strike twice in the same place, and that criminals never return to the scene of their crime – it's nonsense. Armed robbers, in particular, will always return to a job where they have previously had financial success. I once knew a little Glasgow blagger who robbed one particular branch of a building society more than ten times in two years. Simply because, every time he robbed the place, he got away with a good chunk of cash. It became known as his 'lucky' target.

Sean had a rucksack over his shoulder – the 'happy bag' as it is known to blaggers. Inside the happy bag were a single-barrelled, sawn-off shotgun, a couple of baseball caps, two bandannas and gloves – all the kit they would need to commit an armed robbery. They parked Sean's bike down at the end of an alley, a couple of doors up from the bank. Sean and Roberts slipped into the rear of Danny Mac's's car and sorted out their robbery kit, putting on gloves, bandannas around their faces and baseball caps pulled low. Sean ordered Danny to bash the car's horn for three long blasts if he saw anything sussy. The two robbers headed purposefully towards their target.

Coming out of the alleyway and onto the street, the two robbers took a good look around. They were looking for the signs of a ready eye or police ambush, though both knew it would be unlikely because, even if the police were tailing them to the target, they would not have had time to set a proper ambush. The robbers knew that the most dangerous time for them would be when they were leaving the premises after the robbery. This is when the robbers were more likely to become targets for the guns of the Flying Squad; when they were bang-to-rights.

As the robbers walked towards the entrance to the bank, they heard the revving of a motorbike as Vinnie Bradish turned up on his blue Suzuki. Vinnie pulled up on the other side of the street and Sean and Roberts walked over to meet him. It turned out that Vinnie had been riding around looking for a target himself when he noticed his brother and Roberts. Vinnie was eager to come into the bank with them, but they had no spare bandanna or hat for him. Sean told him to ride around the locality and check for Flying Squad.

Vinnie knew that, by doing this security check, he could now lay claim to a share of the proceeds for helping out with the robbery. The fact that Vinnie really did very little except check if there were any police about would not stop him from being charged with conspiracy to rob or attempted robbery if it all came on top. He would be standing in the dock as one of the robbers if they were caught. The gang were all well aware of this so there was never any arguments over who got a share and, to Sean, although the money was a great bonus, the adrenaline rush was what he was really craving.

Sean and Roberts relaxed on a small wall and waited

for Vinnie to report back. Within a couple of minutes, Vinnie rode past them and gave them a thumbs-up. The two robbers pulled their bandannas around their faces and headed into the bank. Sean rushed to the counter and pointed his sawn-off shotgun at the cashiers and loudly demanded the money. Roberts was the doorman on this job and stayed close to the door to make sure nobody left before the robbery was done.

While Roberts was waiting for Sean to fill the bag, he glanced outside and saw a car pull up on the opposite side of the street. Two men jumped out of the car and quickly headed towards the boot and began rifling about in it. Roberts felt the panic hit him like a bucket of ice-cold water down the back of his neck. His pulse and heartbeat quickened and small beads of sweat began to pop out on his forehead. Surely these guys were the police. There were all the hallmarks of Old Bill. Roberts gave a strangled cry. 'Old Bill.' he managed to shout. Sean froze with a bundle of bank notes partway into his bag and looked at Roberts. 'Get the fuck out of here!' Roberts shouted, fighting to keep the panic out of his voice. Sean put the shotgun into the rucksack and both men ran for the door.

Vinnie Bradish was sitting unobtrusively on his Suzuki about a hundred yards from the bank and was surprised to see Roberts and his brother come barrelling out onto the street at high speed. He sat up straight, wondering what the hell was going on. He started his bike and wheeled away into a U-turn before gunning the engine and vacating the area. Sean and Roberts ran to the alleyway where Sean's bike was parked under the watchful eye of Danny Mac. Roberts was in the lead as they headed for the mouth of the alley and Sean called out for him to take the bag. Sean launched the rucksack through the air and Roberts caught it on the run. Once Roberts was in possession of the bag, Sean took a swift right turn and headed off onto a field behind the alley.

The car containing the two suspicious-looking men was now hot on Roberts's trail. It pulled into the alley and headed towards Roberts, who was still running towards Sean's bike. The car had to swerve around the bollards at the end of the alley, which gave Roberts the moment he needed to reach inside the rucksack and produce the shotgun. The car screeched to a halt in front of Roberts and the two occupants jumped out, one speaking fast into a mobile phone. Roberts stood in front of them, pointing his shotgun forwards. 'Fuck off or I'll blow your fucking kneecaps off!' he shouted and cocked the shotgun.

By now he was at Sean's bike. Danny looked shocked but tried his best to pretend he was just a passer-by who had nothing to do with this. He put one hand in his pocket and walked away from the scene, cringing inside for the shot that might now hit him between the shoulder blades if these guys were armed police. Roberts realised that Sean had the key to the motorbike and that he had no way of making a quick getaway. He waved the shotgun at the two men and shouted, 'Get the fuck away!' He was desperate. Suddenly, Sean arrived at a run and jumped onto the motorbike. Roberts kept the shotgun pointing at the two men and jumped onto the seat behind Sean. In a hot second Sean had the engine started and in gear and the bike, carrying the two robbers, was gone in a cloud of dust and exhaust fumes.

The two men decided that having a sawn-off shotgun pointed at their faces was a bit too much and did not follow the bike. Sean rode straight to Ealing Road and The Chequers pub, which he knew quite well. They rode into the front garden of a derelict house adjacent to the pub and Sean parked his bike behind a large hedge. They quickly stripped off their outer garments and strolled out onto the pavement and made their way to a nearby cab office. They could hear the sirens in the near distance. It had been a close call.

Sean was to later find out that the two men who had interfered with their getaway were, in fact, police officers. They were members of the local CID, who had been called to deal with a shoplifter who had been caught stealing in a shop close to the bank. The two policemen were Detective Constables Christopher Jelley and Ralf Kirchel, attending the call in an unmarked car. According to DC Jelley:

On Monday, 3 July, I was on duty dressed in plain clothes, in company with Detective Constable Ralf Kirchel in an unmarked police car. We were sat in the vehicle in the service road outside Sapena Wines, 1217 Greenford Road, Sudbury, Middlesex. I was sat in the front passenger seat and DC Kirchel was in the driver's seat. We were there from about 2.45pm in relation to an inquiry. The premises next to Sapena Wines is a Barclays bank.

It was a clear, hot, sunny day and the area was busy with pedestrians and vehicle traffic. In the mid-afternoon, his colleague DC Kirchel called out, 'I don't believe it, there's a blag taking place,' so the two hopped out to take their batons and CS spray out of the car boot. At the same time, DC Jelley saw two men running out of the bank. He recalled that the first was wearing a white baseball cap and a white top, and that the other male was wearing a blue top.

The two officers hopped back into the vehicle and picked up speed, with one driving and one ringing 999 to alert New Scotland Yard. Then Jelley recalls the suspects heading right, into an alley. Kirchel pulled the car in after them. There was a railway line beyond a fence on the left-hand side. Sean and Roberts both pounded up the alley, but there was no outrunning a vehicle. As the car drew level, Jelley opened the passenger window, intending to spray them both – but things did not go according to plan.

As I was attempting this, I could see three metal poles that appeared to be blocking our route. We slowed down to negotiate these poles and managed to drive through the left-hand side. Whilst doing so, I saw that the male in the white cap was holding a shotgun across his chest. As we negotiated the poles, that male turned and faced us. As we drove through, he levelled the shotgun at us, parallel to the ground from his waist. It was pointed at us and I could see that the barrel was shortened and had a light-coloured wood-type stock. We stopped and I was aware of the other male to my left, somewhere by the grass. I never saw that male again. The male with the gun turned around and jogged off and we followed in the vehicle. Near the bottom of the alleyway on the right side, he again stopped and faced us, pointing the shotgun in the same fashion. He was stood against the tree line. After a short hesitation, we drove past him into Ridding Lane.

DC Jelley also recalled that the man with the gun appeared to be trying to fire, and getting frustrated at its failure to discharge. After briefly losing sight of him, the gun-toting menace then appeared from behind a fence, and this time Jelley was able to see his face – his cap had gone. He had short, dark hair. He was just under six feet tall and of thin build, perhaps getting on for thirty years old. After that, the gunman disappeared, but his white baseball cap was left behind on a grassy verge nearby. DC Kirchel seized it in an evidence bag. Later, as detectives combed back over the area of the chase, a blue scarf and two black gloves were found in the undergrowth near where the gunman had faced down the two police officers.

Meanwhile, the two robbers had gotten a cab to Harlesden, and went into a pub called Gambles. They were well known in the pub and people left them alone as they sat in a dark corner and split the money up. They had managed to grab just over four grand from the bank, which was divided equally among the two of them after taking £300 off the top for Vinnie and £100 for Danny.

Sean was cursing, as he knew that, if they'd had the time, there had been a lot more money behind the counter. Roberts left Sean in the pub and went to a nearby sports shop to buy them new tops.

Once again, they had gotten away, even with the possible intervention of police, and they were feeling invincible. Well, Sean Bradish was feeling invincible; Stephen Roberts was feeling very little except a high from the drugs that he had purchased with his share. The next day, Sean returned to the garden and picked up his bike. Nobody seemed to have got the number plate during the job, but Sean was thinking seriously about trading it in and getting another. As far as Sean was concerned, Roberts had acquitted himself well on the bank robbery – a bit panicky initially but he'd had no hesitation in taking the gun and threatening police officers. Sean trusted him, but only in as much as he might trust anyone whom he considered might be nearly as ruthless as himself in this game. Roberts was not family, but, according to Roberts, this job was the last straw for him. He claimed later that coming so close to being arrested had made him think about giving the game up. He was also worried about leaving items behind that would contain his DNA. How right he was to worry.

CHAPTER FOURTEEN

UP AGAINST THE SQUAD

Like any firm that takes up armed robbery for a living, the Bradish gang knew that there was a distinct possibility that, sooner or later, the Metropolitan Police's 'SO8' were going to be hot on their trail. Special Operations 8 – or the Flying Squad, as they are more commonly known – are responsible for investigating any and all armed robberies in the capital. If you are committing armed crime in London, it is odds-on that the squad are going to get a sniff. They cultivate snouts and grasses as a matter of course, and are always ready to listen to a hot whisper from some toe-rag that might lead to a blag.

The Flying Squad is a branch of the Serious and Organised Crime Command within the Metropolitan Police Service. Formed in October 1919, with a team of twelve detectives, they were originally called the Mobile Patrol Experiment (MPE) and their original brief was to gather intelligence on known robbers and pickpockets.

The MPE used a horse-drawn carriage with holes cut in the canvas in order to spy on their intended targets. Right from the start, the squad had a reputation for sneakiness but were also considered to be good 'thief-takers', and that counted for a lot in the relatively new police force. Most coppers are willing to overlook dubious methods as long as they get their man. The result is what counts.

In 1920, the MPE were reorganised and given the authorisation to carry out duties anywhere in the Metropolitan Police District. This order gave rise to the nickname 'Flying Squad', because they could be all over the place at a moment's notice, regardless of divisional boundaries. This was a major coup for this squad, who were now on a much longer leash than the rest of the Metropolitan Police. They were also given two brand-new vehicles to aid in their new-found working freedom. The first vehicles used by the squad were converted Crossley tenders with experimental radio masts so that they could be in touch with Scotland Yard and each other.

A little-known fact about the first two vehicles used by the Flying Squad is that they gave rise to the common modern nickname for the police. Their original Crossley tenders had the number plates BYL1 and BYL2, which London criminals soon memorised and converted to 'Bill cars' and eventually to 'the Bill' and 'Old Bill'.

The squad really made its reputation as hardened thief-takers, who weren't afraid to put the cosh about themselves. During the Battle of London Airport in July 1948, the Flying Squad heard from an informer that there was to be a robbery of bullion, jewellery and cash from the BOAC (British Overseas Airways Corporation) secure bonded warehouse at London Airport (later to be renamed Heathrow Airport). The informer was actually one of the guards, who had put the crime up to the gang in the first place. It was to be his job to slip a Mickey Finn to the rest of the guards so that they would be ten toes up and catching big zeds by the time the robbery gang arrived. In the event, he had a serious change of heart and instead informed the Flying Squad about the plan. Flying Squad officers then went undercover at the airport, disguised as BOAC warehouse workers. In police records, this was called Operation Nora.

The BOAC robbery was to be one of the most audacious crimes of its day, as the warehouse held £325,000 worth of valuables, including £1,000 in gold bullion and £13,900 in cash. In today's value, this would be the equivalent of around £10 million.

In the early hours of the morning of July 28, a covered lorry pulled up outside the warehouse and several well-armed robbers jumped out to carry out their business. It is not certain how many actual robbers were there that night, and estimates vary between eight and fifteen in the gang. They were led by a well-respected thief and hardman called 'Big' Alfie Roome who, in his younger days, had been known as the 'Ilford Kid'. The job itself was rumoured, very strongly, to have been planned by Jack 'Spot' Comer, 'the King of the Underworld' according to his press coverage, but 'Spot' was never arrested in connection with this job. Also on the work was Sidney Cook, who was dressed in BOAC uniform and drove the vehicle to the job. The other gang members involved were an assortment of east-London villains and hardmen, including Billy Benstead, Bertie Saphir, Franny Daniels, Samuel Ross, John Wallis, Teddy Machin and Teddy Hughes, who, at 48, was the oldest of the gang. Each of the gang, except Cook, wore gloves and stockings over their heads – the first time this disguise was recorded as being used in a robbery. The gang also carried a variety of weapons, including iron bars, lead-weighted coshes and large shears. Cook had a starting-handle as a weapon.

Once the gang had got into the warehouse, they were soon to find out that nobody had been drugged and that Flying Squad officers had taken the place of the workers. Once this became apparent, all hell broke loose and the Battle of London Airport began. One of the crooks shouted, 'Let's settle these geezers!'

According to records, they were met with a cry of, 'We are police of the Flying Squad. Stand where you are!' from an Inspector Roberts.

Realising that their plan had been rumbled, the gang made a dash for the door, but they found their exit blocked by yet more police. One of the gang is said to have shouted, 'Let's kill these fucking swine!' During the brawl that followed, the second-in-command of the Flying Squad, DCI Bob Lee, had his scalp split open with an iron bar that was wielded by 'Big' Alfie Roome. Detective Sergeant Fred Allen was stabbed in the thigh with a broken water carafe, Detective Sergeant Donald MacMillan had his nose broken, Detective Sergeant Mickey Dowse had the bones in his hand shattered as he tried to ward off a blow from a crowbar and Detective Inspector Peter Sinclair had his arm broken in a similar way. The fight spilled onto the concrete apron outside the warehouse and, pretty soon, eight of the robbers lay unconscious as they were beaten with police truncheons.

Billy Benstead and Bertie Saphir managed to escape the melee and leg it to safety. Teddy Machin got chased by several police officers into the surrounding darkness. He fell into a ditch and knocked himself out and was completely missed by the police pursuers. (Teddy Machin was not so lucky in 1970, when he was blasted with both barrels of a sawn-off shotgun through the window of his house in Canning Town and died.) Franny Daniels managed to crawl underneath a lorry and hang on, intending to drop off and roll away when the lorry came to a halt, but the lorry drove straight into the yard of Harlington Police Station. Luckily for him, Daniels was able to leg it.

The gang appeared at the Old Bailey on 17 September 1948, where they pleaded guilty to conspiracy to rob while armed. The Recorder of London, Sir Gerald Dodson told them: 'One can only describe this as the battle of the BOAC, for that is what it degenerated into. It is a thing honest people regard with terror and great abhorrence. A raid on this scale profoundly shocks society. You went prepared for violence and you got it. You got the worst of it and you can hardly complain about that'. The gang members were sentenced to between five and twelve years' imprisonment respectively. As Dodson sentenced 'Big' Alfie Roome to ten years, the gang leader started to sob uncontrollably. After this, Alfie was ostracised in prison and shunned by other criminals for showing weakness in the face of the enemy. This is how criminal legends are made and then broken. When he was finally released from prison, he found that his wife had started an affair with a younger man, so Alfie attacked the pair in an effort to kill them and then poisoned himself. Both his wife and her new lover survived but Alfie did not.

Due to this epic battle and the convictions that followed, the Flying Squad were fast going down in folklore as a force for criminals to reckon with. Every member of the team received commendations from the commissioner. The Battle of London Airport cemented the reputation of the Flying Squad as tough, violent thief-takers in the minds of the London underworld. Some would say that the Flying Squad have been doing their best to try to live up to that reputation ever since.

By 1956, the Flying Squad made a thousand arrests per year for the first time. In 1978, at the height of the armed-robbery boom years, the name of the squad was changed to the Central Robbery Squad, but they were still commonly known as the Flying Squad. During the 1970s, the squad was involved in a number of serious scandals involving bribery and corruption. In 1977, the squad's commander, Detective Chief Inspector Kenneth Drury, was convicted on five counts of corruption and sent to jail for eight years. Twelve other officers were also convicted and many more resigned rather than face the music. A slight whiff of corruption has hovered over the squad ever since.

It is well known among the armed-robbery fraternity

that the Flying Squad love nothing better than to catch a team in the commission of the crime. In the 1970s, when armed robbery reached epidemic proportions countrywide, the police realised that their policy of nicking robbers before they had actually committed the crime was costing them convictions. Even if they nicked a couple of likely lads in a stolen car, wearing masks and holding a bag of weapons, there was still a good chance that a decent silk could convince a jury that his clients were merely unfortunate victims of circumstance. After all, there had been no actual robbery. At best, for the accused it would be a 'not guilty' and, at worst, a shortish sentence for theft or possession of firearms. So the Flying Squad decided to change their MO. Armed police will say that there was never a 'shoot-to-kill' policy when it came to armed robbers – that is their official line, but they claim that they 'shoot-to-stop' and, if someone gets killed by that, so be it. So, in effect, the police do shoot to kill. An ex-police firearms expert, Steve Collins, revealed in his book *Good Guys Wear Black* that shooting to kill was what they did.

In my humble opinion, the exact moment that the Flying Squad realised they could get away with practically anything was after the shooting of Stephen Waldorf in London in 1983. Stephen Waldorf was a twenty-six-year-old film editor who had been misidentified as a wanted armed criminal called David Martin. On 14 January 1983, Stephen Waldorf was the front-seat passenger in a bright-yellow Mini being driven by his friend Lester Purdy in Earl's Court London, when the car was ambushed by several armed Flying Squad officers. The police surrounded the Mini when it stopped at traffic lights and, without any warning being given, DC Peter Finch opened fire with six rounds at the passenger side, while DC John Jardine fired five shots through the rear window of the vehicle then moved to the side and fired two more shots into the car. DC Finch then leaned into the car and aimed his revolver between Stephen Waldorf's eyes and, apparently, said, 'OK, cocksucker,' then pulled the trigger. Fortunately for Waldorf, Finch had already fired off all of his bullets and the revolver was empty.

Finch then proceeded to drag the wounded Waldorf from the car and pistol-whipped him in front of horrified pedestrians and drivers. Stephen Waldorf was hit six times and severely wounded in the head and stomach, with a bullet also going through his liver. The terribly wounded man was then handcuffed in the gutter. It was not until much later that the Flying Squad found out they had made a big mistake and had tried to kill the wrong man. A total of thirteen shots were fired, at almost point-blank range, six of which struck the innocent Stephen Waldorf, but he had eleven bullet holes in his clothing where other shots did not pierce his body. Truly, he was lucky to be alive.

It has always been rumoured in the criminal fraternity that the reason for the eagerness of the police in wanting to kill David Martin was more than a little bit personal. Not only had he shot and wounded a police officer but there is also a story that, if true, would explain the savagery of the broad-daylight attack on Stephen Waldorf on a London street in rush hour. It is said that the Flying

Squad had had the flat of David Martin's girlfriend under surveillance for a couple of days and saw only a tall, good-looking female leave and enter the premises. Eventually, they decided to give her a pull to find out if she knew where Martin was. Two Flying Squad men knocked on the door of the flat and were invited in by the lady of the house. After a bit of questioning, she made tea for the two officers and, as they drank it, produced a pistol from her bra and forced both policemen to handcuff each other to a pipe in the kitchen. Then David Marin – for it was he dressed in women's clothing and make-up – left the police officers in a somewhat compromising and embarrassing position by inserting one of their truncheons into them. Martin then made his escape, leaving this grotesque tableau for their colleagues to find.

David Martin was eventually captured by the Flying Squad in 1982 as he tried to escape down a London tube tunnel. He was jailed for twenty-five years after a trial at the Old Bailey. Two years later, he was found hanged in his cell at HMP Parkhurst, on the Isle of Wight.

Another major milestone in the evolution of the Flying Squad was the Acton Post Office robbery. The robbery of the Post Office at Old Oak Common Lane, Acton, West London, was committed by a Yardie gang armed with semi-automatic pistols on 14 December 1988. The gang were under surveillance by the Flying Squad at the time, though they did absolutely nothing to prevent the crime, merely instigating a gunfight with the gang on the streets after the robbery.

For some time, the Flying Squad had been after

better firepower than the Smith & Wesson five-shot .38 revolvers that they carried as standard. They argued that the weaponry that the robbery gangs were carrying far outstripped the power and capacity of their weapons. The Acton robbery was to be just the demonstration that would illustrate their case perfectly.

Several of the robbers, including Brian 'Bunny' Beckford and Andrew Clarke, ran from the Post Office and, when challenged by armed police, proceeded to run and fire off their semi-automatic weapons as they went. Mayhem.

The police fired back, hitting the robbers in several places but failing to bring them down. In the end, it was a police officer with a baseball bat that put an end to the gunfire by stepping from cover and hitting Beckford across the shins, bringing him down and disarming him. Two of the robbers were shot, as well as two police officers.

The fact that the robbers had the Squad outgunned, and did not succumb after being shot, made the argument for the Squad to get more up-to-date and powerful weaponry a matter of urgency. Two of the robbers, Beckford and Clarke, were sentenced to imprisonment for over twenty years each at the Old Bailey in 1989. The Flying Squad got shiny new weapons and the game was on. Instead of poxy Smith & Wesson five-shots, they were now issued with 9mm, seventeen-shot Glock pistols. Plenty of stopping power.

From the mid-1980s, the police's penchant to shoot first and ask questions not-at-all was well in effect. Many London robbers were to breathe their last while staring down the barrel of a police pistol. Tony Ash, David Ewin, Mark Nunes, Dennis Bergin, Micky Flynn, Nicky Payne, Jimmy Farrell, Terry Dewsnap, Kenny Baker and many more were shot dead by police – either the Flying Squad or PT17 (who worked closely with the Flying Squad) – with little or absolutely no warning. Criminals are not stupid, and nor do they live in vacuums. These shootings became very well known and discussed in the armed-robbery fraternity. This meant that it was common knowledge among criminals that the Flying Squad were now operating a shoot-to-kill policy in order to reduce the number of armed robberies on their patch. This also meant that some robbers would now be more mindful of using their weapons when confronted by police. The streets of our cities became more dangerous places.

The readiness of police squads to shoot first and ask questions not-at-all was all too evident during the 1990s. At this time, members of a well-known south-London crime family, supposedly the successors to the Krays, were heavily involved in cash-in-transit robberies. The Arif brothers – Deniz, Mehmet and Dogan – had been involved in major crime such as armed robbery and drug dealing since the 1970s. The brothers had a reputation as one of the major crime syndicates in London and were well known to the police.

In November 1990, Denis and Mehmet Arif, Tony Downer and Kenny 'Big Head' Baker (who was married to the Arif's sister) had plans to rob a Securicor van on its stop at a petrol garage in Woodhatch, near Reigate in Surrey. The gang were professionals who had carried out many such robberies together and all knew the drill. The van was carrying £750,000 in cash, and the Arifs were going to hijack the whole van, rather than just rob the guard. Unfortunately for the gang, the Flying Squad, along with their usual armed escort of PT17 officers, had caught a whisper that the job was to go off. They set up a ready eye around the proposed target and waited to ambush the robbers in the commission of the crime.

Police watched as the Securicor van arrived in the garage forecourt and two guards got out in order to pick up tea and sandwiches. Suddenly, a pick-up truck with the back covered by a large tarpaulin pulled into the garage. The tarpaulin was thrown back, revealing the robbery gang wearing Ronald Reagan masks and toting sawn-off shotguns. They proceeded towards the van and got hold of the security guards, and forced the rest of the crew inside to open the doors by threatening to kill their colleagues. Baker's brother-in-law, Mehmet Arif, was wearing an Afro wig and had his face blacked up as a disguise. He was also carrying a handgun. The crew inside opened the van doors and Deniz Arif climbed into the back with one of the guards. Tony Downer took the other guard into the front of the vehicle and got behind the wheel. Baker, his work done, headed back to the pick-up truck, where he and Mehmet were to follow the Securicor van to a bit of safe ground nearby where they could clear out the cash.

Suddenly, a couple of unmarked police vehicles screeched into the forecourt and blocked the exit. One vehicle stopped next to the pick-up and a PT17 officer carrying an MP5 sub-machine gun jumped out and tried to pull a surprised Kenny Baker from the truck. The police officer claimed that, as he pulled open the door of the pick-up, Kenny Baker was pointing a gun at his face. The police officer fired two shots at Baker, one of which hit him in the stomach, and the second hit Mehmet Arif, who was in the driver's seat. A second PT17 officer, armed with a rifle, ran to the front of the pick-up and fired through the windscreen and hit Kenny Baker in the face just below the eye. Baker was dead before the echo of that gunshot died away. It was later established that the first shot in the stomach would have killed him anyway.

Meanwhile, the robbers already in the Securicor vehicle, Tony Downer and Deniz Arif, could only watch the scene unfolding before them. Tony Downer, still sitting in the driver's seat of the Securicor van, raised his hands but he was still holding his gun. Another PT17 officer fired five shots at Downer but, because of the armour plating and bullet-proof glass on the windows, none of the shots penetrated the van. Downer was lucky to be alive. He quickly dropped his gun and jumped out of the van and laid on the street face-down in surrender.

Deniz Arif, who had climbed into the back of the van, was now trapped in the vehicle. The security procedures kicked in and automatically locked the back of the van. Deniz had to wait there, surrounded by armed police officers, for the police to either shoot him or nick him. After some discussion with the trapped Arif, he decided to give himself up, but nobody knew how to get him out. Eventually, a rather svelte member of the squad wriggled his way into the van through the narrow cash chute and arrested Deniz Arif. The police officers then, working on phone instructions from Securicor, were able to open the escape hatch on the roof of the vehicle.

Once again the police had shot to kill a professional armed-robbery team who they had never been able to catch or convict in a court of law. It is no wonder that word went around the armed-robbery fraternity that the Flying Squad and PT17 had declared open season on villains.

During a shootout during a Post Office robbery in Brockham, near Dorking in Surrey, in 1992, police ended up shooting and injuring not only the robbers but also members of the public in their eagerness to pull the trigger. The police officer in charge of the operation stated that, while he was sorry for any injuries to the public, 'Sometimes it is necessary to fight fire with fire.'

A year later, in 1993, a Flying Squad sergeant named Michael Stubbs was hit in the head by a 9 mm round fired from a Skorpion sub-machine pistol during a high-speed chase through Blackfen, South London. Security-van robbers Steve Farrer and Anthony Pendrigh were being pursued after snatching a cash box containing £17,000 in cash. The Flying Squad had them under surveillance and immediately gave chase, but the robbers – who were very well armed owing to Farrer's father being a legal firearms collector – were not going down without a fight. Farrer leaned backwards out of the getaway car and fired off a thirty-two-shot magazine at the pursuing Flying Squad vehicle. DS Stubbs was hit in the head by one of the 9 mm rounds ricocheting off the road. Farrer and Pendrigh pleaded guilty to the attempted murder of police officers, armed robbery and possession of firearms and ammunition (including possession of a Spetz automatic shotgun used by the Russian Special Forces and needing a special licence from the Home Office for its possession), and were both jailed for eighteen years.

Due to these developments in the 'enemy camp', the Bradish gang became very adept at anti-surveillance – driving around roundabouts three or four times and doubling back on themselves in order to spot any police who may have been tailing them. The mobile phones they used during robberies were unregistered throwaways. They never spoke to anyone about what they were up to unless it was other members of the gang. They were a tight unit, but even the tightest unit can have a weak spot and, in this case, it would turn out to be Steven Roberts.

Vinnie Bradish was a very smart and watchful criminal; he liked to plan ahead and forever kept his eyes open for anything out of the ordinary. Sean, on the other hand, was a bit more reckless and relied on his own speed, wits and propensity for action and violence to keep him out of trouble. Sean loved to go and rob 'on spec': just pick up a gun, jump onto one of his motorcycles, or even a mountain bike, and ride around looking for targets. That way, he figured, the police would have to be great at following him or have to be mind-readers to know what he was up to, and he used so many anti-surveillance tricks that the police would have had to have been sitting inside his exhaust in order to keep up with him.

Knowing, as they did, about the MO of the Flying

Squad, the Bradish gang were well aware that, every time they stepped out on the pavement to pull off a bit of skulduggery, it was odds-on that, if the police were involved, there was a good chance they could have ended up bleeding their lives into a dirty gutter. But still they carried on with their lawless lives, albeit in a more watchful and prepared manner. Sean Bradish would have no trouble pointing loaded firearms at the police, and maybe even pulling the trigger, if his liberty was on the line. And this was to be proven in short order.

CHAPTER FIFTEEN

ANGRY

On Wednesday, 12 July 2000, Vinnie was in a pretty bad mood. He couldn't exactly put his finger on what was exactly wrong – it was a combination of things. As he was having breakfast that morning, he'd been watching the news and one of the lead items had been about the loyalist marches in Northern Ireland, 12 July being the start of the marching season, and, being a Catholic of close Irish descent, it pissed him off to see the bowler-hatted brethren with their big drums and flutes basically rubbing their ancient victories in the faces of the indigenous Irish population. 'Fucking eejits,' he mumbled under his breath. It didn't help that he had slept badly and had a pain in his neck. He decided that what he needed was to go and chore a large chunk of cash and go on a bit of a spending spree.

He met up with Sean and Roberts and they were both up for a bit of work. Sean fancied doing a Thomas Cook shop, as they were always great for a bit of summer cash with everyone paying for their holidays around this time, but they couldn't decide which one so they decided to cruise around on their bikes and look for a likely target. The lads knew that they were on the Flying Squad's radar and had spotted a couple of police tails in the preceding days. The close call while robbing the security van in the grounds of the hospital had made Roberts wary about robbing vans out in the open, and he was paranoid enough with all the coke he was sniffing. But money was needed and Vinnie was in the mood to stick two fingers up at authority, so off they went.

Sean was riding a K-reg Honda CBR 600 and Vinnie was riding a blue Suzuki 600, with Roberts riding pillion. Roberts had a JD Sports string-necked bag, with the gun and disguises inside over his shoulder. The lads cruised around north-west London, checking all the usual places. Vinnie wanted to do a security van and experience told them that, at this time of day, they were likely to find one. Sure enough, as they rode down Cricklewood Broadway, they spotted a white Securicor van parked at the kerb outside a building society. It was an Abbey National and the guard was just getting out. Vinnie was in the lead and signalled to Sean to follow him around a turning just along from the van. There was a brief discussion about the target.

Roberts immediately started making excuses not to rob the van – he claimed he had a 'bad feeling' about this one, which Vinnie countered by remarking that he thought Roberts's arsehole had gone and that he'd had a 'bad feeling' about nearly every job they'd done. Sean wasn't bothered. He sat on his bike and waited for the decision to be reached. Vinnie was not in the right frame of mind to really listen to anything Roberts had to say; he was doing it and that was that. Vinnie snatched the happy bag from Roberts, nearly pulling him off the bike in frustration at wanting to get going. Using his crash helmet as a disguise, Vinnie walked quickly onto the Broadway and pulled a double-barrelled, sawn-off shotgun from the bag.

In a statement made to the police a few months after this robbery, Roberts claimed that Vinnie snapped the shotgun open in front of him and checked that the gun was loaded. Vinnie laughed this off when I spoke to him and he stated: 'The guns were always loaded before we set out on a bit of work. You'd have to be a right amateur prick to be snapping open guns out on the street to check if they're loaded! The only reason Roberts said that was because, when he rolled over, the police wanted maximum bang for their buck. If he could assure them that I was checking the ammo like I was looking to shoot as many people as possible, it would indicate to the jury at trial that I was a lot more dangerous than I appear to be.'

Vinnie called for Roberts to follow him to the van. Sean pulled his bike out of the side road and parked in the car park of a McDonalds just up the road from the van. From here, he sat on his bike and kept watch on the van and the building society. As Vinnie, followed by Roberts, approached the van, they saw the security guard was on his way out of the building. Vinnie quickened his pace and brought the sawn-off up level with the guard's body. Behind his visor, Vinnie saw the guard's eyes widen almost comically as he realised what was going on. The guard tried to turn on his heel and head back into the building but Vinnie was quicker; he was up on the guard before the man could move any further. Vinnie grabbed him by the collar and dragged him into the outer vestibule of the building society. Roberts jumped into the line of the electronic doors to stop them sliding closed and trapping Vinnie in the building. The guard started shouting, 'Help! Robbery! He...'

Vinnie yanked down hard on his collar and spun him around until he was crouched over with the barrels of the shotgun pointed at his neck. He let go of the cash box and put both his hands straight in the air in order to show compliance. Vinnie pulled his own crash-helmet visor up and stepped back. He pointed the gun at the guard's chest and shouted, 'Open the fucking box! I'm not in the mood for you today! Come on, open that fucking box!'

The guard knew this guy was serious and he feared for his life. He fumbled the key from his waist and unlocked the box. There was a grey cash sack inside the box and Vinnie snatched it up. He stood staring at the guard for a long second, during which the guard was sure he was going to be shot by this angry robber. Then Vinnie turned away and walked briskly out of the vestibule.

Vinnie and Roberts ran around the corner to the Suzuki and piled on. Vinnie had handed the JD Sports bag to Roberts and he bagged up the gun and the cash bag and slung it over his shoulder. They rode past the

McDonalds and Sean rode out and tailed them. When they were far enough away from the scene of the crime, Sean pulled level with Vinnie and told him to head for the Holiday Inn in Brent Cross to hide up.

Vinnie paid for the room on the ninth floor of the hotel and the three robbers counted up their haul. There was £20,000 in cash in the security bag and this was enough to lighten Vinnie's bad mood. They split the money between them and set off for Brent Cross shopping centre for a spend-up. They would normally buy a completely new outfit after a robbery and dump the clothing they had been wearing – usually trainers, tracksuits, jeans and shirts. They knew that forensics played a large part in police work, so they didn't want to give the police anything to work on. So a distinctive top or pair of trainers that might be pictured in CCTV had to go straight away. The clothing would usually be pushed into a random bin. In reality, the only thing that perpetrators leave behind after most robberies is CCTV images, whether from a banking institution or street cameras, and, as long as their faces are covered, the only thing the police will have to go on are the CCTV images and any distinctive or unusual clothing the robbers might have been wearing.

After this robbery, Roberts spent a lot of his share on drugs; his habit was becoming ever more voracious and, with it, his paranoia. He started to really believe that they were going to get caught and spend the rest of their lives in prison. He was starting to hate Sean and Vinnie, but Sean in particular. He knew that Sean was the more dangerous and unpredictable of the two brothers. He had seen his violent rages up close. He still shuddered inside when he thought of what Sean had done to the suspected sex-offender in their local. But Stephen Roberts felt trapped. He needed money in order to feed his drug habit but robbing with the gang was the only way he could see of getting his hands on enough cash to supply his needs. He was thinking more and more about what he had heard regarding those who gave their all to the police in order to avoid prison. Yes, he knew it was a big step and that his life would be priced by his former criminal friends; they would make sure that there was good money available for anyone who would be willing to maim or even kill him. Those were the rules of the criminal world that he had willingly joined.

He thought of the amount of times that he had sneered at suspected grasses and agreed with his comrades that they should be given the worst treatment possible. In prison, where informers are attacked in the most horrific ways, such as by having boiling water and sugar thrown in their faces, his life would not be worth living. What Roberts was starting to get interested in was the witness protection programme. He knew there was one in America and now he wanted to find out if such a thing existed for British informers.

CHAPTER SIXTEEN

WITNESS PROTECTION

The UK's nationwide witness protection programme is run by the UK Protected Persons Service (UKPPS), which is responsible for the lives of around three thousand people. UKPPS is part of the National Crime Agency (NCA). Until UKPPS was put together in 2013, the protection and resettlement of witnesses was the responsibility of whatever police force was dealing directly with the informants. The person or persons who are going into protection are told that they will be giving up everything; passport, national insurance number, driving license are all replaced by documents in the new identity supplied by the police. Often they must leave members of their family behind as they disappear into their new life.

The protected person/persons will be allowed to pack one suitcase themselves, but the police will pack up all of their left-behind property and take it to them a couple of days after they arrive at their secret safe house. They will usually be held at a temporary safe address while a final destination is being sorted out for them. In some serious cases, the witness/witnesses can be housed abroad, but this is quite rare. The protected person is given £300 per week in pocket money while they are awaiting their final destination. They are given a cover story that they must stick to and are usually temporarily housed in a town far from where they have originally come from for a period of up to six months. This is so they can familiarise themselves with the town or area that will be the birth place on their new documents. Once they are familiar with the area, they will then be moved to their destination with the cover story now in place.

Within reason, people entering the witness protection programme are allowed to state a preference for where they would like to live the rest of their lives. Some people have no preference and leave it entirely to the police. They are usually given a final choice of two addresses in their new area. The UKPPS work to the idea that those who enter the programme will not be worse off financially than they were before they entered, but nor will they be better off. Of course, with some of the major criminals who enter the programme, they will have been living far above their legal means before entering and the programme makes no concession to supply them with anything coming from ill-gotten gains. However some naysayers in the criminal world would class the whole witness protection programme as 'ill-gotten gains' for traitors and informers.

Perhaps the most depressing thing for a former career criminal entering the programme is giving up the excitement of their criminal lifestyle. Or, as American organised-crime informer Henry Hill remarked when he was relocated to small-town USA, 'Now, I'm an average nobody... I get to live the rest of my life like a schnook.' There is no more free money, no more fast cars or motorbikes, no more adrenaline-infused action and violence, and, for some, life just becomes a bore. Certainly, Henry Hill couldn't hack the inaction and even went on to commit more crime when he was part of the witness protection programme.

As for Stephen Roberts, there is no doubt that he is an adrenaline junkie as well as an illegal drug junkie. You cannot spend years putting your life and liberty on the line daily, dodging the authorities and stealing huge amounts of cash without getting addicted to it. Will he ever be tempted back into the criminal world? Who knows for sure? And, even if he does go back to crime, he could never hope to regain the criminal heights of his previous life. He would be recognised and dealt with. The world of the armed robber is relatively small and not much goes unnoticed by those who inhabit it.

Barring some spectacular comeback, Stephen Roberts, one-time gunman, robber, junkie and supergrass is gone for ever.

CHAPTER SEVENTEEN

THE ROBERTS 'UNDERCOVER COP' THEORY

Speaking to Vinnie Bradish about Stephen Roberts is like opening a can of concentrated theories, beliefs and absolute hatred. It is understandable that those who have been informed on and put into prison for many years by a trusted associate will not be happy, but you can see the naked rage in Vinnie's eyes when he talks about Roberts.

When Vinnie was eventually nicked, on the word of Roberts, some months after Sean had been arrested and remanded for the Royal National Institute for the Blind (RNIB) security-van robbery he was remanded into prison with Sean and the rest of the lads. And finally he got a chance to see the statements that Roberts had made to the Flying Squad after his own arrest. He was shocked at first at how much of a turncoat his one-time accomplice had become. But, after he and Sean had studied the

Roberts' statements, they started to notice things that did not seem to add up.

For a start, when Roberts was first interviewed after his arrest, he was asked about a recent robbery and, although he was co-operative, he could not give any real details. He claimed his memory was not good and that he had abused himself with so much drink and drugs that everything was a bit of a haze. After he decided to become a supergrass, his memory had an amazing restoration and he could suddenly remember what colour top Sean had been wearing on a robbery five years previously. In question after question during his interviews, it was almost as if the famous hypnotist Paul McKenna had given him an intense crash course in total recall. The question might be, 'Steve, can you remember what car was used on the robbery of the Woolwich building society on the morning of 2 April 1994?' Quick as a flash Roberts would give the make, model, year and number plate of the vehicle in question. This, even though hundreds of robberies were carried out over a five-year period and Roberts, also by his own admission, had stolen over one hundred cars to use on robberies. He could remember the details of every robbery, every car he stole, the clothing worn, the amount of cash taken, the firearms used, where every gun was kept, the lot.

As Vinnie told me, 'Either he was keeping fucking notes for a five-stretch or the police supplied him with all the information before he was interviewed.'

According to Vinnie's theory, Roberts was an undercover agent for the police long before he met up with the Dirty Dozen, and he was tasked with getting into their gang and bringing them down. To back up his theory, Vinnie points to the fact that almost everyone that Roberts worked with on a criminal enterprise ended up arrested soon after. Drug dealers who refused to supply him or to whom he owed money were suddenly getting raided. His enemies – and there were a few, even before he publicly declared himself a wrong-un – found their premises being raided by the police. Anyone who Roberts knew had a gun, a cannabis grow or a bit of stolen property stashed pretty soon found the police kicking through their doors. The fact that the Flying Squad had been following Roberts and the Bradish brothers around for nearly five years, saw them committing robberies and acting in very suspicious ways, and yet never moved in to arrest them, did not seem right. Even when they were blatantly throwing security-dyed furniture and fittings out of the top window of Sean's girlfriend's house, the police did nothing except take a video and some pictures of it.

Vinnie says:

OK, they know a security box is stolen from the Post Office and that it is opened in the flat and explodes, covering everything in red dye, yeah? The next day they are plotted up in an OP across the road from the flat and take a video and photographs of us getting rid of the furniture and fittings into the front garden of the gaff. And that's it? Correct me if I'm wrong, but the dye-packs they use to try and protect cash-in-transit have got a kind of DNA-style imprint, just like the Smart Water they use in some banks and Thomas Cook shops, yeah? So why didn't they come and nick us and take a sample of the dye-stained carpet or curtains? Bang! If they were really interested in nicking us, that would have been their obvious move, don't you think?

Vinnie also tells me about a time towards the end of their robbing days when he, Sean and Roberts were going to rob a bank that they had plotted up. On the morning of the job, Roberts asked Sean to drop in at an army-surplus store as he wanted to buy a boiler suit. Vinnie and Sean laughed at this idea as it had come out of the blue. 'A fecking boiler suit!' hooted Vinnie. 'What, are you going to do a few odd jobs round the bank while we empty the tills. You fecking eejit!' But Roberts insisted that he needed a boiler suit for this robbery. The Bradish brothers refused to stop at a shop to get one, as they had their usual disguises.

It was only after Roberts spilled his guts to the Flying Squad that Vinnie began to run things over in his mind, looking for anomalies in Roberts' behaviour, and he remembered the boiler-suit incident. He told me:

I should have been a bit more on the ball with that, because it now seems obvious that Roberts wanted to wear a boiler suit on that bit of work so that he could easily be identified by the armed police who were going to be there to shoot me and Sean. It's not rocket science: if they couldn't nick us, shooting us dead is the next best thing for Old Bill. It's not like they don't have previous for it. In the end, we blanked that bit of work because it looked a bit too sussy. We always had a rule that, if one person doesn't feel right about the job, we would usually abandon it. Sometimes instinct is all you've got to go on and, for a serious criminal, that can mean the difference between being shot dead, serving bundles of years in the big house, or walking around with the sun on your face. To this day, I think the police were up for shooting us and I believe Roberts was in collusion with them to make this happen.

Another plank in this theory about Roberts' wanting the brothers dead is that he was terrified of Sean and did not like Vincent. Vinnie told me, 'I had a little thing going on with Veronica, Roberts' girlfriend. It was nothing serious, just a one-off thing. But, as you would expect, Roberts got a bit upset about it. I knew he didn't really like me after that but, to me, he was no real loss. He was more Sean's pal. But he had also fallen out with Sean because my brother set up home with one of his ex-birds. Towards the end, me and Roberts barely tolerated each other.'

Another suspicious move, according to Vinnie, is that the RNIB security-van job – the one where Sean was finally nicked – was Roberts' own bit of work. Vinnie said:

'He was the one who discovered it, he was the one who plotted it up, watched it, timed it and then offered it to Sean. The thing is, on the day that Sean decided to actually do the proffered job, Roberts suddenly gets cold feet and decides he wants to take a back seat on it. Sean spoke to Roberts on the phone the night before and the latter said he "didn't fancy it" because he had misgivings about the getaway from the job. He had been shouting about that job for weeks and, if Roberts hadn't trumpeted the job so much, Sean would never have bothered with it and he would not have been nicked that day.'

That aside, with the rate at which this gang were committing robberies, the law of averages says they were bound to get a tug at some stage. But I have to agree with Vinnie about the many little anomalies in the statements and behaviour of Stephen Roberts, so could he have been an undercover police operator all along?

I very much doubt that. For a start, I had spoken to people who knew him before he joined the Dirty Dozen and, unless he had been in the police since the age of twelve, it was highly unlikely. He could though, as Vinnie proposed, have been recruited as a paid informer during the late 1980s and been given the mission of infiltrating the gang. Knowing how the police have worked over the years, putting undercover police officers and agents into politically motivated protest groups, like the animal-rights group and others, anything is possible. Police agents actually lived the same life as their targets, integrating groups so deeply that some police operatives ended up having children and living with their intended targets. So it is not beyond the realms of possibility that, while Stephen Roberts was taking vast amounts of class A and B drugs and terrorising financial institutions of London, he had been doing it with the full knowledge and implied consent of the authorities.

But the police are not talking, and Roberts has disappeared like a puff of smoke into the ether, so the chances of finding out for sure are minimal at best.

Vinnie, though, is convinced that right at this moment Roberts is working his way into another criminal enterprise with the aim of bringing it down in the same way he brought down the Dirty Dozen gang. Maybe he's right.

CHAPTER EIGHTEEN

THE POLICE CHIP IN

If you commit armed robbery in London, you already know the Flying squad are bound to be interested. Of course, the police had been putting members of the gang under intermittent surveillance ever since Jimmy Doyle was arrested. The police suspected that they had never rounded up all the members of Doyle's gang, but the fact was that, when 'Gentleman' Jim's mob went down, the Bradish brothers were still just rookies at the robbery game. They had learned from Doyle and the senior members of the gang; they had been his apprentices, in a way. They hung around with the older members, listened to the stories of their exploits and witnessed the benefits of their lifestyles. Sean and Vinnie Bradish had learned their trade and were only too happy to carry on once Doyle and his firm were out of the picture.

In the autumn of 2000, the police launched Operation Embrace, which involved following and gathering evidence on the Bradish brothers' little gang with a view to finally arresting them. A briefing on the gang was held at 6am in Finchley Police Station and chaired by Detective Inspector Cummings and Detective Inspector Shanks. Photographs of all the gang members were passed around, along with photographs and details of the vehicles that they had access to.

Throughout the day of 5 September 2000, undercover officers stalked Sean and Vinnie Bradish through the streets of London. The police were hoping to catch them in the act and either arrest them or shoot them dead if the circumstances called for it.

At 2.02pm, police officer Andrew Michael reported seeing Sean and Vinnie on their motorbikes entering the Rose Hill roundabout in south London. They took the exit for the A217. At 2.44pm, Sean's grey BMW car was under obbo by several plain-clothes officers as it was parked, unattended, in the car park of a gym in Gander Green Lane.

The surveillance continued and an observation post was set up in a top floor flat facing the Co-op car park on Wrythe Lane. From here, police had the Rose Hill roundabout under observation, which was used frequently by the Bradish brothers, as their bolthole in south London was just up the road and they would have to travel over the roundabout. Even though the Bradish boys were from north-west London, they committed some of their robberies in south London and, in particular, the Morden area. They had a sister who lived close to the St Helier Hospital and often visited south of the river. The boys liked being in deep south, as they felt free away from their home area, where everybody knew them. South London was a place where they felt they could relax a little bit more than on their home turf. Little did they know that the police had discovered their trips south and had set up watch on them here as well.

From their observation post, the police logged every movement of the brothers and Steven Roberts and it must have been a long and boring job. For example, DC Gary Murphy of the Flying Squad states that his day began with a briefing at 6am, followed by an arrival to his observation post at 9am. Constant radio contact would have been kept up with the loggist [police officer who writes all observation logs], whether or not any meaningful observations could be recorded. Finally, DC Murphy later recorded in painstaking detail:

At 11.39am I saw a motorcycle, K763 EYH, turn left into the Co-op car park, from the direction of Rosehill roundabout. I was aware that Sean Bradish was riding the motorcycle. At 11.43am I again saw this motorcycle, coming from Rosehill roundabout and travel past the car park entrance and continue towards St Helier Hospital. At 11.54am I saw Vincent Bradish walking in Wrythe Lane towards the roundabout. At 12.20pm I saw Vincent Bradish and Sean Bradish walking in Wrythe Lane and passing Superdrug. At 1.58pm I saw motorcycles K763 EYH and J963 DUC in Wrythe Lane towards the roundabout.

On the whole, this was typical of a police surveillance operation. The idea was to catch the suspects in the act, hence the early start, around 9am, and the 4.30pm finish. Most banking institutions and cash-delivery services will typically operate between these hours. The police did not want to nick these boys in the evening while they were watching TV in their slippers. That would not be exciting for a jury. They wanted them on the street, guns and cash bags in hand. They had to get convictions, otherwise all their expensive surveillance work would have been for nothing.

Since at least 29 August 2000, the police had surveillance on the Surrey address of Sean Bradish. According to the logs, they watched every move that Sean made during daylight hours. They watched him with his kids, they watched him as he took his dog for a walk on Sutton Common, they recorded the make and colour of every item of clothing he wore, and their hearts raced a little faster whenever he met one of the gang or went out on his motorbike, as they hoped he would be going to commit a crime. They were out of luck. According to Sean and Vinnie, they had long been aware that they were being watched for quite some time, but that had not stopped them from committing their crimes.

Vinnie told me that he had been very suspicious of the motives of the police in watching but not arresting them.

I couldn't figure it out. We knew they were on us. We see them enough and, let's face it, when you are at it every day, you kind of learn to see a bit better.

Maybe it's the paranoia, but you seem to pick up on little inconsistencies, things that just kind of feel out of place, you know? And I'm thinking to myself, 'What the fuck is the story with this mob? Are they just going to let us go on reefing the fuck out of London, or are they going to nick us, or what?' We weren't that worried, to be honest. I mean, as far as we knew, they had no actual eyes on us when we were actually working and we always masked up on a job so we knew there couldn't be any decent photos of us – nothing you could use as evidence, I mean. We didn't keep any of the tools around us. The guns were always in safe places that couldn't be tied to us – safety deposit boxes under false names or lockers in gyms that we hired with fake ID. We knew it would be very hard for them to prove we had done anything at all. But, of course, at that time, we didn't know that Roberts was the viper in our nest.

In October 2000, the police watched Sean as he carried out a recce on a cash-delivery van at the Co-op Superstore in Surrey. Detective Paul Leon Russell observed Sean on his motorbike enter the car park wearing a dark-blue hooded top, blue jeans and white trainers with dark flashes. Sean parked the bike towards the back of the car park and sat quietly observing the scene. Around five minutes later, DC Russell records that a gold Audi car, index number E885 HPV, driven by Vinnie Bradish, came around the roundabout and entered the same car park. The Audi passed Sean and pulled into an empty space nearer the Superstore. Within the next ten minutes, a white Securitas cash-delivery truck pulled into the car park and parked near the entrance to the Superstore. The guard got out of the van and went to get a supermarket trolley, and both guards began loading money bags into the trolley. Sean Bradish got off his bike and slowly walked through the car park, watching the van all the while. For a moment, there was panic among the three undercover police officers who were observing the scene. They were certain that the van was about to be robbed. This would not be the first time that the Bradish boys had committed one on the spur of the moment but, luckily for the guards and the police, it was only a recce. Sean had plans to rob this van at some point in the future; he had no weapon on him today and neither did Vinnie. The police watched as both Sean and Vinnie separately left their vehicles and walked around the area, watching every movement of the Securitas guards.

DC Russell noted the details of the brothers' movements: 'Sean Bradish looking intently at the cash delivery vehicle. 1.49pm, Sean Bradish walks back towards the exit, looking at the cash delivery over the railings. 1.53pm, Sean Bradish turns around and walks back to the car park whilst still looking through the windows of the Superstore at the guard inside. 1.56pm, Sean Bradish back on motorbike and out of car park.' He then notes that, when the Securitas van leaves the car park, it is being followed by Vincent Bradish in the gold Audi. During this whole time, the police were taking photographs of the robbers, which they could later use as evidence if the case ever came to court. DC Russell is officially listed as a police photographer.

In a statement from 8 June 2000, DC Russell records following Sean Bradish down Harlesden High Street, where he videoed a meeting between Sean and Vincent Bradish, Stephen Roberts, Steven Wall and Danny Mac. Later that same day, DC Russell followed Sean Bradish to the Safety Deposit Centre, High Road, Wembley. At this stage, the police had no clue where the gang kept their guns and did not know that there were five loaded firearms in a security deposit box, along with around five grand in stolen bank notes. But now they became interested in the Safety Deposit Centre at Wembley, and this interest was to have an effect on another major criminal with no links to the Dirty Dozen gang whatsoever. Except a passing resemblance to Sean Bradish.

CHAPTER NINETEEN

TOMMY THE BOXER

Sean Bradish, like other major criminals, needed a safe place in which to hide not only his ill-gotten gains but also his sizeable collection of illegal firearms. Sean knew that most of the gang would be able to weather a raid by the police, as there would be very little evidence to connect them to anything, but that meant keeping the tools of the trade someplace where the police would never find them. He heard about the Safety Deposit Centre in Wembley from one of the drug dealers on the manor, so Sean hired a box in the mid-1990s using fake ID and stashed anything incriminating, such as guns or marked money, in the box.

Once the Flying squad caught onto the fact that Sean had been visiting the centre on regular occasions, they decided to set up on OP on the gaff. They guessed that whatever Sean had in his box was going to be very useful in their getting a conviction, and they wanted whatever it was.

Unfortunately – or, perhaps, fortunately if you were one of the police involved – a major Irish criminal, drug dealer Tommy 'the Boxer' Mullen, had the same idea about security deposit boxes and decided to hide some of the loot he was making from crime in the one at Wembley. It was probably the worst decision he ever made in his life.

Tommy Mullen was an ambitious young Dublin criminal, who was also a very good boxer; in fact, he was an international boxing champion by the age of eighteen. Growing up on the mean streets of North Dublin, Tommy was surrounded by the effects of a heroin epidemic that had gripped Ireland since the early 1980s. Cannabis, cocaine and heroin flooded Ireland under the control of the various Irish crime gangs, who really came to the fore in the years running up to the Good Friday Agreement that put a stop to 'the Troubles' in the Northern Irish province. Mullen became mixed up with a north-side gang whose speciality was heroin and he soon realised that the amount of money in that game was phenomenal. Pretty soon he was searching for places to hide the loot.

Tommy was becoming so well known as a criminal in Dublin that, in June 1996, less than one hour after newspaper reporter Veronica Guerin was shot dead on the orders of Dublin's crime bosses, the Garda were kicking in the door of Tommy Mullen's house in Artane, north Dublin. Guerin had interviewed Tommy for a newspaper article, which was to be one of the last she wrote, and Tommy had publicly branded her as 'vindictive'. When the police arrived at his home, Tommy was relaxing there and police quickly ruled him out of their investigations.

Tommy told me that the reason he came to London in the first place was because he had received serious threats from a Dublin organisation called Mothers Against Drugs (MAD), and from Republican paramilitaries. The backlash against drugs – but heroin, in particular – was pretty intense. MAD, which consisted of many older men, women and ex-paramilitaries, would 'march on' anyone suspected of being a heroin dealer. To 'march on' meant to bring a huge protesting crowd to the dealer's home or business in order to discourage them from dealing drugs to their children. They usually 'discouraged' the dealers by wrecking their houses, beating the dealers with baseball bats and hammers and generally giving them plenty of stick. MAD was set up because the communities felt that the police were doing nothing about the problem, so the ordinary people decided to take things into their own hands.

In Tommy's case, he'd had a visit from some rather more serious-minded and brutally violent individuals with heavy links to the borderlands of the North, who beat him and put him into a coffin, which they then threatened to nail closed and throw into the rushing waters of the River Liffey if Tommy did not depart *tout de suite* for pastures greener, preferably England. Tommy was tough. He could take a decent punch and he could throw down like the champion boxer he was, but there is no fighting an organisation with a background of bombing, assassination and torture. Tommy was on the boat to England the very next day.

Once in London, Tommy used his old contacts from Dublin and elsewhere to set up a heroin business. He teamed up with a Turkish heroin dealer named Turhan Mustafa and, pretty soon, they were raking the cash in hand over fist. For a while, everything was swinging for Tommy. Then he decided that the best place to hide his newly acquired loot was in a safety deposit box, where all the rich people in the world hide things that they have no wish for the authorities to know about.

With the help of a little whisper from the Irish Garda, the English police were soon taking an interest in the coming and goings of this rich, handsome, young Irishman, who seemed to be wealthy way beyond his visible means. The drug squad had Tommy 'the Boxer' Mullen firmly in their sights. They were just waiting for him to make a mistake.

The trouble for Tommy came in the fact that he looked remarkably like Sean Bradish. Both men were over six feet in height, proportionately built and both had shaved heads. It was while police were watching the Wembley Safety Deposit Centre that they spotted what they thought was their target going into the building and then walking out with a heavy holdall. Thinking it was Sean carrying a bag of guns for a robbery, the police pounced. Instead of Sean Bradish, armed robber with a bag of guns, they ended up with Tommy 'the Boxer' Mullen, drug dealer with a bagful of cash.

When Tommy was searched by the police, they found

£1,000 in cash in his jacket pocket and £105,000 in his holdall. There was a further £92,000 and several passports in his name left in his safety deposit box.

Tommy was found guilty at Snaresbrook Crown Court in north London of conspiracy to supply Class A drugs and was sentenced to eighteen years' imprisonment. As a footnote, me, Sean, Vinnie and Tommy were all on the same wing at Whitemoor prison some years later, and Tommy held no grudge about being mistaken for Sean.

CHAPTER TWENTY

'HE SHOT A DUCK...'

Speaking to Vinnie Bradish about Stephen Roberts is like tiptoeing through a minefield. Sometimes his face flushes with the anger and betrayal of his one-time confederate and he looks ready to explode; other times, he just looks resigned to the fact that nobody can be trusted. I asked Vinnie about any violence displayed by Roberts, as I had noticed in various evidence statements that Roberts always seemed to be the one pointing the guns at security guards, customers and, occasionally, the police. Just like the original supergrass, Bertie Smalls, it turns out that Roberts was probably the most violent and vicious of this gang of violent armed robbers.

'Roberts and Steve Wall were two-of-toast,' Vinnie told me.

One time they attacked a couple of mates of mine with a machete and an air gun. This was long before we were working together, but I remember he was a vicious bastard, swinging the machete like he wanted to kill the guy. I think he was a bit of a psychopath, to be honest. He loved hurting things and people. I remember one time we were going to deliver a couple of guns to somebody for a bit of work and Roberts was carrying a little girl's gun – one of them sawn-off .410 shotguns – and I was taking the piss out of him for it, you know, just joking around a bit.

So we get out of the car and Roberts' is fuming – you can see it all over his ugly face. We were in a bit of a rural area and there was a small pond with ducks mooching around it. So Roberts, not being fucking brave enough to challenge me on my piss-taking, just turns around and shoots this duck that's waddling by the pond. I couldn't believe it: this fucking psycho shot a fucking duck to prove how hard he was! I went fucking mad at him. We're trying to be a bit discrete, what with the guns on board and the police surveillance, and this fucking head-the-ball is shooting a defenceless bird. I know he didn't really like me before that incident but, after I gave him a proper bollocking, I could see the hate in his eyes.

The fact that Roberts was a violent man is beyond dispute. By his own confession, he committed some pretty violent acts when he was engaged in robbing drug dealers before he joined up with Sean Bradish. The trouble is that, on the whole, drug dealers and the inhabitants of crack-houses will not go to the police, even when they have been beaten, stabbed and robbed. Apart from the fact that informing is against the so-called criminal code, they would probably not be believed by the police and just laughed out of the station.

When he was on cocaine – which was the majority of the time – Roberts had a very short temper and would be snappy and aggressive to all around him, except Sean and Vinnie. He was very frightened of the two brothers and careful not to aggravate them too much.

CHAPTER TWENTY-ONE

BINGO

Armed robbers are forever on the lookout for a prize, the prize being an easy job with plenty of cash. So it was no surprise that, when on his travels in south London, the ever-vigilant Sean Bradish came across a Securicor van picking up cash from a bingo hall in Rosehill in April 2000. The Mecca bingo hall was close to the Rosehill roundabout, near a flat the brothers had in the South London suburbs. Sean had been heading for a meeting with the rest of the gang in Wembley when he noticed the familiar blue van slipping into a rear car park. He stopped his bike and walked closer to watch the routine of the guard. He watched from behind the wall of the car park as the guard sauntered into the hall, seemingly without a care in the world. This one was there for the taking and Sean had to stop himself from just jumping the guard on the spot. He noted the day and time of the pick-up in his memory and carried on about his business.

This job would be one of many that members of the gang looked at and may or may not get around to doing.

As a professional armed robber – as in someone who does it as a full-time job – you will find yourself mentally noting the times and movements of every security van you see. Every premises that holds cash, jewellery or anything of value that might be worth robbing will be considered and parked in the back of the mind for possible future investigation or action. Your eyes mark everything as you walk down the high street – cash deliveries, lack of security, possible undercover police officers. It is like your brain cannot switch off from this stuff. You go to buy a stamp at the Post Office and, while waiting in the queue, you are working out in your mind how you might rob the place, where the money is kept, what the best getaway route is, how close the police station is, and a million other details that are of interest when you are a villain.

Sean watched the pick-up from the bingo hall, filed it away in his mind and then let it rest. Two months later, in June 2000, he happened to be in south London and he and Vinnie were at a loose end. Sean suddenly thought about the bingo hall and he and Vinnie decided to rob it. They had to wait until the next day, which was Thursday, 24 June, the day the van was due, but it was now a prominent target. The next morning, the boys decided to use Vinnie's blue Audi to get to the job, and they had a black BMW that Roberts had stolen for another job at their disposal, which would be used as the getaway vehicle. Both Sean and Vinnie knew the area very well, thanks to the location of their hideout flat, and given that some of their relatives also lived in the area. Sean liked to do the occasional robbery in this part of London, as it was a break from Wembley, Harlesden and Cricklewood, which, to be fair, they had been rinsing for a five-stretch. Sean always felt a bit more relaxed when carrying out a bit of skulduggery away from the manor.

The first time Sean had noticed the Securicor van at the bingo hall, it had been 12.30pm. So the boys, complete with a double-barrelled, sawn-off, 12-gauge shotgun, bandannas, baseball caps and shoulder bags, arrived at the bingo hall in Vinnie's Audi just before 12pm. The stolen BMW was parked in a side street off the main roundabout and within running distance of the target. The plan was for Vinnie to be the wheelman, waiting in the car for Sean to do the work and then get him away with the prize. Sean, as was his wont, would do the actual robbery alone. Sean didn't mind; he had worked a van on his own a couple of times in the past. In fact, he relished being out there at the sharp end, gun in hand. It was an addiction to Sean, just like it can be for a lot of men who commit armed robberies on major cash targets.

Sean walked off to recce the area around the bingo hall and make sure there were no undercover police lurking around and waiting to ambush him. This was always a concern for robbers, as you never know if another robbery team has already looked at the target and is planning the work, therefore presenting the risk that the police might have followed that team and be waiting. It sounds unlikely but I can assure you that it does happen. The police even have a name for it: 'Crossing Targets'. Sean was quite sure that he and Vinnie had lost their own Flying Squad tail, as they were experts at anti-surveillance moves. They knew that the police were watching them but were equally sure that they had never been observed committing a robbery because, surely, the police would have then had to arrest them. Little did they know that the Flying Squad had built up quite an impressive file against the Bradish boys and their little firm. They knew a lot more than the boys gave them credit for.

The blue Securicor van rolled into the bingo hall car park just before 1pm. It was a standard cash-in-transit van with a two-man crew. On that day, the crew consisted of Shabu Abdulkareem, who had been employed by Securicor for eleven months, and Michael Sogee, who had worked for the firm for nearly five years and was far more experienced than Abdulkareem. Guard Sogee had made all of the pick-ups and deliveries prior to 12pm, when he swapped places with Abdulkareem and got into the rear of the van. Sogee was more of an action man than his work partner, and he would be the guard more likely to put up a fight if there was an attempt to rob them.

Sean, crouched down behind a parked car to the rear of the bingo hall, watched intently as the guard climbed out of the van and walked into the bingo hall. He noted that the guard seemed unaware – bored even – and did not look closely at the surrounding area. He was carrying a smoke box, which Sean could tell by the padlock on the outside of the box. The smoke box is designed so that if there is an attempt to open it red smoke bursts out, marking the attempted robber and his location for all to see. The amount of smoke that comes from such a small device is surprising and the red plume can be seen for some distance. Sean cursed under his breath. The last smoke box he'd taken had been a pain in the arse to get open and the money had ended up dyed a bright crimson. Sean knew that the bank notes could be washed in a bath using a solution of white spirit and biological washing powder, but it was a time-consuming chore.

Sean pulled the sawn-off shotgun from the duffle bag he had over his shoulder and flicked the safety catch off. The gun contained two 12-gauge Ely birdshot cartridges and he had another four in the side pocket of his jacket just in case. He slipped his black bandanna around the bottom half of his face and pulled his black baseball cap low over his eyes. All anyone would be able to see of his face would be a narrow strip between the bridge of his nose and his eyebrows. He waited until he saw the guard coming from the bingo hall and then left his crouch and crossed the ground to the guard in a fast lope.

Abdulkareem later told the police that he was wearing uniform and a protective helmet. He put two cash bags and two coin bags into the smoke box, and locked it with a padlock – a small kind of the combination variety. But, as Abdulkareem recalls:

When I was given it this morning, I knew the box was defective. Inside, the bingo hall was open and there were a lot of customers playing, or about. As

I left the hall, I did not notice anything unusual. I walked towards the van but had to go around a parked car near the van. As I got within a couple of yards, I noticed a man running towards me from my right-hand side from the general direction of beside the bingo hall. I noticed he was carrying a black bag and the lower half of his face was covered by a black scarf. He was also wearing something over his head – I think a baseball cap. When I first became aware of him, he was about a van's length from me and, as he got closer, he said, 'Drop the box.' He didn't shout, just said it in a normal voice. I thought he was joking at first then I noticed he was holding a shotgun in both hands, which was pointing towards the box I was carrying. He repeated, 'Drop the box, or I'll blow your head off if you don't.'

Naturally, Abdulkareem dropped the box. His assailant picked it up and turned, ran back in the direction he had come from. Deciding it was too dangerous to follow, Abdulkareem told Michael Sogee, who was inside the van, what had happened. The pair called the police straight away, who arrived within about three minutes.

Michael picks up the story:

I ran in the direction the man had run. About forty–fifty yards into the alley I saw the cash box had been discarded. I kept running into St Helier Avenue. I saw across the other side of the dual carriageway a man walking down St Helier Avenue towards

Morden. He was carrying a sports bag. I crossed the dual carriageway and approached the man. I said, 'What have you got in the bag?' As I was talking to the man, I was aware of another man to my right. He had a sawn-off shotgun, which he pointed at me. He said, 'You black bastard.' He then chased me across the carriageway. He stopped in the central reservation. I ran back to the van.

In the event, Sogee was lucky that he had not been shot dead. As far as I am aware, security companies have a policy not to put their employees in danger and Sogee was acting on his own instincts. I believe the only reason that he walked (or ran) away from that incident unharmed is because, by the time he reached them, Sean had passed the shotgun to Vinnie and was sorting the money bags out. Perhaps Sean Bradish would not have been as patient with being chased by Sogee as Vinnie was. Luckily for all involved, we will never know.

The robbery netted the Bradish brothers just over £15,000 in cash. It came to the attention of the police nearly a year later, once Stephen Roberts started singing for his supper. Even though Roberts was in no way involved in this robbery, he knew enough about it, apparently, including remembering who did the job, where it was, how much was stolen, the date and time, the car that was used and the clothing worn. Which is quite strange, unless the police had given him the details of the robbery before he made his statement. He claims that the Bradish brothers told him about the robbery when they were all having a drink with friends sometime after the robbery, but, even if they did happen to mention it, there is no way these two – especially Vinnie, who did not trust him – would tell him every single detail, down to the clothes they were wearing. It just does not seem credible.

CHAPTER TWENTY-TWO

ON SPEC

Every day was a robbery day for the Dirty Dozen and, if anything viable was spotted, they would not hesitate to hit the target.

One summer morning in July 1998, Vinnie and two other members of the gang, who have never been convicted, were sitting outside a pub in Acton, just having a few drinks and enjoying the sunshine, when they. They watched the van, just out of habit at first but then more keenly as they noticed that the guard seemed a little bit lax in his security checks. He seemed to be distracted and was not looking at his surroundings as he should have been. This set off an alert in Vinnie, who turned to his companions and raised an eyebrow. Surely this was too good to pass up. The three men were experienced armed robbers and knew the robbery routine like it was tattooed on their eyelids. Vinnie told me, 'We were always up for it, and me and the boys couldn't believe this was happening right in front of us. It was like fate had said, "Here you go, lads, little present for you."'

On the spur of the moment, the three of them decided to rob the van. The first thing they did was to quickly bag the glasses they had been drinking from and put them into a duffle bag that was being carried by one of the men. They didn't want to leave any tell-tale DNA, just in case it was pointed out by anyone that they had been drinking across the road before the job went off.

DNA was dangerous. In 1983, two south-London robbers hit a security van in Camberwell and stole £60,000 in cash but had to abandon their getaway car. They decided to duck into a pub to avoid the hue and cry and, as the police scoured the area for them, they had a pint each and just sat in the corner of the pub like they were regulars. Unfortunately for the two robbers, they left their fingerprints on the glasses they had been using. The landlord of the pub – an ex-police officer – on hearing the sirens and police activity and spotting the two slightly sweaty and furtive-looking men, decided to keep their glasses to one side. He later passed them to the police and, on this evidence, both men were convicted of armed robbery and jailed for twelve and fourteen years, respectively. Another robber, known to both me and the Bradish gang, was convicted on DNA evidence when he shouted in the face of a security guard during a robbery and left a speck of saliva on the visor of the guard's helmet. You can never be too careful when it comes to leaving DNA behind.

Vinnie and his companions moved quickly. They

spread out and approached the security van from different angles. One of the hallmarks of a Bradish brothers' robbery was the use of baseball caps and bandannas as disguises. Vinnie always had a bandanna on him, just in case he spotted something too good to resist, and he quickly wrapped this around the lower half of his face. One of the other men had a small lock-knife on him, which he pulled out the blade on. Vinnie and the other man made do with their fingers in plastic bags to give the appearance of guns.

The three men timed their stroll to the van so that, just as the guard came out of the supermarket with the second cash box, they were confronting him. 'Drop the fucking box or I'll blow you into the middle of next week!' Vinnie growled at the surprised guard. At first, the guard thought somebody was having a joke with him and he smiled. That was until the third robber came from behind him and wrapped a tight arm around his neck. The guard panicked and swung the cash box at Vinnie and gave a strangled yell.

The guard in the back of the van saw what was going on and immediately set off the alarm. This was a repetitive wail followed by a loud automated voice that said, 'THIS VAN IS UNDER ATTACK. PLEASE CALL THE POLICE.' As the alarm went off, the guard seized his opportunity to break free from the robber's grip and legged it. The guard ran across the road, still clutching the cash box, and the three robbers spurted after him.

The guard was in a panic and ran through the first open door, which happened to be a clothes shop. He slammed the door and leaned on it so that the robbers couldn't get in. The people in the shop panicked and started screaming, trying to get out of the back. The guard held the door with all of his strength as the three robbers crashed their body weight into it.

Outside, Vinnie could see the guard's panicked and sweaty face through the glass as he strained to keep them out. The alarm was still going off as the rear guard in the security van spoke to the police on his radio system. Vinnie could see shoppers and passers-by gathering on the opposite side of the road to watch. He dropped onto his arse and powered both feet into the lower panel of the door two or three times. There was the loud crack of splintering wood and, suddenly, the panel of the door popped out of its frame. The guard left the door and ran to the rear of the shop and ducked down behind the counter.

The three robbers entered the clothes shop and Vinnie shouted to the now terrified guard, 'Throw the fucking box out or get shot, mate. Your choice.' The guard, realising that he had nowhere left to go, pushed the cash box out from where he was hiding and flung it so that it slid across the floor to the robbers. Vinnie snatched the box from the floor and the three robbers fled the premises.

The robbers split up once back on the high street and ran in different directions. Vinnie carried the cash box and was determined not to let it go. Sirens were approaching the area, but Vinnie ducked down side streets and around corners. There was no way he could get back to his car, as it was parked in the pub car park in the opposite direction. He took off his jumper and wrapped it around the cash box as he ran. He rounded a corner and saw a woman alight from a black taxi and quickly jumped into the back before she had finished paying her fare. Vinnie directed the driver to drive to the Stonebridge estate, and then sat back in relief as the taxi coasted out of the area.

Vinnie took the cash box to Sean's girlfriend's house. The front door was open, so he ran straight into the house and upstairs to a back bedroom. Sean wasn't home but the girlfriend was cleaning up. Vinnie told her to phone Sean. He then set about breaking into the cash box. He didn't know whether the box contained a tracking device so time was of the essence. He snapped the padlock off the box with a large screwdriver, but then heard the tell-tale pop and buzzing of a dye-pack going off. Immediately, the room was full of red smoke, which would instantly mark anything it touched. Vinnie flung the windows open as fast as he could in order to let some of the smoke out. He was coughing like a hundred-fag-a-day smoker as the smoke went down his throat and into his lungs.

Sean's girlfriend started banging on the bedroom door and screaming at Vinnie to get out of the house and take this lunacy with him. Vinnie, by now bright-red skin and clothing, managed to get the box open and found £20,000 in dyed bank notes. He stuffed the money into a holdall and wrapped the now slightly smoking cash box in binliners. He phoned a local cab driver, whom he sometimes used to ferry him about, and asked the cabbie to pick him up. He walked straight past Sinead, saying, 'You might want to get rid of everything out of that bedroom. Tell Sean I'll see him later.' And then he was in a friendly cab and on his way to safer climes. Once he was far enough away from the house, he asked the cabbie to pull over and he dumped the cash box in a roadside bin. He phoned his two comrades and told them to meet at one of their houses to carve the money up.

Though they had managed to get away with the cash, it was not a very lucrative robbery. When Sean saw his back bedroom, he was not best pleased, so Vinnie and the boys had to give him £2,000 to cover the damage. Around £3,000 of the cash was singed or dyed beyond use, which left £5,000 each for the boys. Unfortunately, due to the exploding dye-pack, most of this money was also dyed. The trouble with dyed money is that it is really easy to spot, and a lot of retailers will report it straight away, knowing it could only have come from a robbery. There is a way of cleaning the money, but it is a slow and finicky process. Leave the money to soak for around forty-eight hours and most of the dye will float off, but you then have to fish each soaking bank note from the solution and hang it up to dry, after which the notes will need to be ironed. Instead of going through all this, Vinnie had a better idea.

He phoned Stephen Roberts and asked if he had any dodgy motors at hand. Roberts had a recently stolen Honda with false number plates, so Vinnie got him to drive the car around to him. They didn't mention anything about the robbery to Roberts because, by this stage, Vinnie was starting to get suspicious of him. Vinnie told me:

There was definitely something dodgy about the geezer. I couldn't understand how, after nearly every robbery we did together, he would have some pre-arranged appointment to go to, like dinner with his bird or meeting his mate... mate. The thing was we were doing most of those robberies on the spur of the moment – on spec – so how was he arranging these appointments if he never knew when he'd be available? At this stage, it was only a suspicion on my part. If I'd known... but I decided to distance myself a bit from him. This is when I started to think, 'Well, he's Sean's mate, not mine.'

Before Roberts arrived with the stolen Honda, the boys sorted out a couple of hundred quid in notes that were only slightly dyed on the edges. Vinnie slipped this cash to Roberts. In the criminal world, it does not matter whether you like someone or not, you still give them a 'drink' for their troubles, and Roberts was no exception. Once Roberts had given them the car and stood around shooting the shit for ten minutes, the boys called him a cab. When Roberts was gone, they bagged up the worst of the dyed bank notes and climbed into the Honda and headed for Cricklewood Broadway to put Vinnie's plan into action.

On a sunny Thursday afternoon, Cricklewood Broadway was crowded with throngs of shoppers, pedestrians and schoolchildren coming home from school. Wearing bandannas around their faces and baseball caps on their heads, the three robbers drove down the Broadway, launching handfuls of dyed bank notes out through the sun roof and windows of the car. The crowds went wild, chasing and grabbing this free-floating cash. They distributed over £3,000 to the lucky people of Cricklewood and, at the same time, covered themselves to spend the rest of the dyed cash. By distributing the cash in this way, it would soon makes its way into the tills of the local businesses and, if Vinnie or the boys ever got a pull for having dyed money, they could point to the fact that almost everyone in the area also had some and that it was actually being thrown from a car by some kind strangers. At worst, they might be charged with 'stealing by finding'.

It was not until two years later, when Sean and Vinnie were sitting in HMP Belmarsh going through the statements of supergrass Stephen Roberts, that they realised the Flying Squad already had an OP overlooking Sean's house and that they had filmed him and his girlfriend throwing out all of the security-dyed furniture, carpets and curtains. They had traced the robbery where the box had originally been robbed, but still they had not bothered to nick anyone or seize any of the evidence before it disappeared into a landfill site. Curious.

CHAPTER TWENTY-THREE

THE BEST LAID PLANS...

The long running and lucrative robbery career of Sean Bradish was due to the fact that he had no real or detailed plan. He was the master of chaos. Instead of sitting down with his confederates and working out every detail of each job and the getaway, he relied on the element of surprise and the supposed randomness of his actions. It was almost like he was contemptuous of the kind of *Oceans 11* type approach to crime, where choosing a team and spending weeks building up to a robbery was the template. Sean chose the people he worked with, relying on his own instincts. The things he was looking for in his criminal partners were the same things he prized in himself: plenty of bottle, determination and a lack of empathy for others. And rather than building up to a robbery over several weeks, he would jump up on the spur of the moment and take down one of the targets he kept stored in his brain. As Stephen Roberts put it to his police handlers, 'Sometimes he would just jump on a mountain bike with a shotgun in his backpack and go looking for somewhere to rob.'

Having said all that, there were also times when Sean did deviate from his template of chaos and randomness, and this was usually at the prompting of his brother, Vinnie.

One such case came in one of their robberies in June 1999, in Croydon. The robbery had been put up by one of the gang members as a possible target because he had read in a local paper it had been robbed before and that the take had been over twenty grand. This would be a nice payday for a three-man team. Sean and Vinnie drove to Croydon to take a look at the target and noticed how busy the footfall and traffic was around the Barclays bank. That part of Croydon is a high crime area and there is plenty of police presence in the area. The gang had struck a target in such circumstances before, but on their own manor, where they knew every short cut and back alley for a getaway. The real sticking point with the Croydon job was the parking. The bank was close to a tram stop and on a one-way street with no parking and regular traffic wardens and police traffic patrols.

While carrying out their recce on the target, the boys noticed that a Post Office van was able to park up on the pavement very close to the bank. They watched the postman, in his uniform, park his van on the pavement and then walk around the shops and businesses delivering the mail. Vinnie smiled. He had a plan. They would have to steal a Post Office uniform and van.

He decided that they would take a Post Office van from the other side of London to use in the Croydon job. He immediately got in touch with a car thief he knew in Harlesden and told the man what he needed. He did not go to Stephen Roberts because, by this time, Vinnie did not really trust him following the duck-shooting incident. Vinnie later told me that Roberts had been very close to getting his skull cracked over that incident. Vinnie had absolutely no qualms about smashing Roberts in the face with a gun butt; he loved animals and did not like to see them treated badly, especially by a 'gobshite like Roberts'. The Harlesden car thief, thinking he might have an in with the Bradish brothers, immediately went to work.

A postman, at Harlesden postal depot, told police about making his deliveries on 15 June 1999:

I returned to the depot at about 10am that morning to reload the van for the second delivery. I parked the van in the rear yard of the depot, which has open gates to Harley Road, NW10. I got out of the van and left it open with the keys in the ignition and took a couple of parcels into the depot, which I had been unable to deliver that morning.

When I came back out to the van, no more than five minutes later, I noticed it was missing. I looked around the area to make sure that no other postman was playing a trick on me but couldn't find the van. All that was left in the van was my possessions. I had left my Post Office knee-length blue jacket. In this were my house and car keys. Also, in the front of the van was my mobile phone, left on the dashboard, and a Tesco's carrier bag, which contained ham rolls and a pint of milk, and 200 Superking cigarettes. A few days later, I became aware that the van had been found somewhere in south London.

When the van was brought back to the depot in Harlesden, everything that belonged to that postal worker was still in the vehicle apart from the Post Office jacket.

Now that Vinnie's car thief had done his job, the boys decided to put their plan into action the same day. It was a pretty simple plan and the Post Office van and postman's uniform were essential to give them a smother while they robbed the bank. The brothers packed up their robbery kit of two sawn-off shotguns, a pair of glasses for Sean to wear with his Post Office jacket and baseball caps. They drove the stolen van across London from West to South and arrived in Croydon at noon. The real postman had already made his deliveries in Croydon, but they were counting on nobody really noticing because Post Office vans and postmen are ubiquitous on the streets of London and nobody gives them a second glance.

Vinnie was driving the van and he pulled it up onto the pavement in the same spot that they had seen the real postman park. Sean, already wearing the stolen Post Office jacket and a black baseball cap and glasses, had a Post Office bag slung over his shoulder containing a sawn-off shotgun. He wore flesh-coloured surgical gloves and so did Vinnie. Vinnie stayed in the driver's seat of the stolen van and Sean stepped out onto the pavement. Just as they had hoped, nobody even looked twice at the van – it was an everyday sight.

Sean walked casually up to the entrance of Barclays Bank and into the relatively hushed banking hall. He quickly noticed that only one of the tills was in operation. There were only two customers in the bank: a middle-aged man and a younger woman, who was being served. Nobody even glanced at Sean; it was like the Post Office jacket was a cloak of invisibility. He walked up to the counter and took his shotgun from the shoulder bag. He tapped the young woman at the counter on the shoulder and indicated that she should move aside. He pointed the shotgun at the lone cashier, Sharon Coombes, and told her to start putting the cash into the counter chute. The cashier smiled at first, thinking this might be some kind of joke, but Sean quickly disabused her of that notion by banging the gun on the glass screen. 'Get the fucking money up or I'll shoot you in the face!' There was a loud gasp from the customers. Sean turned to the man and pointed the shotgun at him. 'Get over in the corner and keep your fucking mouth shut!' The two customers scurried to the back wall.

The cashier, now realising that she was in a deadly serious situation, began to pull wads of bank notes from her till. She piled just over £3,000 into the counter chute, which Sean snatched up and put in his shoulder bag. When the chute was empty, Sean indicated with the shotgun. 'Open the other tills,' he growled.

The cashier was terrified and shook her head. 'I don't have the keys,' she said, sobbing.

Sean knew there was more cash there and he was loathe to leave without it. 'Get someone out of the back with the keys,' he shouted. He knew there were other bank workers there; he could see their silhouettes and hear their panicked voices.

Sean banged the screen hard with the barrels of the shotgun and shouted loud enough for the hidden bank staff to hear him. 'Get out here and open these tills or I'll shoot them all!' He knew that these staff would have already raised the alarm and that he didn't have long before the police would arrive on the scene. Nobody in the rear of the bank seemed willing to get involved with to an armed man, and Sean knew that, short of firing off a shot, he had reached an impasse. It was time to cut his losses and get the fuck out of Dodge. With one last growl at the terrified cashier, Sean turned on his heel and walked quickly out of the bank.

Vinnie had the engine of the stolen Post Office van running and, as soon as Sean was aboard, he pulled off the pavement and out into traffic. Nobody in the bank would have been able to see the getaway vehicle, and nobody on the street had seen anything suspicious, so Vinnie did no shrieking wheel spins or panicky driving. The van blended into traffic and was gone, leaving behind some very upset and tearful victims.

The brothers dumped the van soon after their getaway and ordered a cab to take them towards Morden, where they had their safe flat. They were both disappointed at the take and, to Sean, it proved his point about doing things on the spur of the moment; planning this job had got them very little reward. Sean decided that he would continue with his own random methods.

It would be another ten months before the gang struck at a target in this part of London again. That was one of Sean's random targets. He targeted the HSBC on Chipstead Valley Road, on 12 April 2000, threatening to shoot a customer named Joanne Redmond. According to evidence, Sean shouted, 'Give me the money. Hurry up or she gets it in the head!' as he held a Magnum revolver to the terrified customer's head. He escaped with over £5,000 and was pictured later that evening with Vinnie, toasting his success with champagne in the lounge of the Holiday Inn hotel in Sutton.

CHAPTER TWENTY-FOUR

TRACKING THE BLAGGERS

The Flying Squad were playing the long game with the Bradish gang. They decided to use every weapon in their considerable arsenal to gather as much evidence about the movements and associates of the gang as possible. A lot of the public do not realise what sort of technology the police can use in their surveillance operations. For example, a law was passed back in 1991 that gave the police the powers to break into an innocent person's house or business premises in order to drill through walls and skirting boards and plant fibre-optic surveillance cameras, and spy on their neighbours. They could do this if the people they were surveilling were part of 'organised crime'. For the purposes of the Act, 'organised crime' was defined as 'two or more persons conspiring to commit crime.' So just think about that for a moment. Imagine you and a friend are in your home and talk about the possibility of stealing something or cheating someone and, if that conversation was overheard by or reported to the police, you would be deemed part of 'organised crime'. The police would then be entitled, if they so wished, to break into your neighbour's home, without their knowledge, in order to spy on you. Seems a bit draconian.

Another thing that specialised police squads seem to use quite frequently is phone taps. A few years ago, if a criminal were to accuse the police of tapping and taping his phone calls, it would be greeted by incredulous laughter, as phone tapping was thought to be the province of secret agents and James Bond novels, but these days, with the advent of the ubiquitous mobile phone, it is much easier for the police to do. They also tap landlines if need be. In the 1990s, when I was heavily into the world of armed robbery and undercover police operations, I noticed that the landline in my flat had a faint echo on the line every time I spoke on the phone. I was telling a friend of mine – a major drug dealer who had experience of undercover police operations – about it and he smiled. 'The way to find out for sure,' he told me, 'is don't pay the bill and see how long it takes the phone company to cut you off. If the police are getting intel from your line, they will never allow it to be closed.'

I decided to follow his advice and, sure enough, even though I did not pay the phone company a single penny, my phone stayed operational for over nine months, until the day after I was arrested. And, sure enough, when I reached trial at the Old Bailey, the prosecution entered a series of taped phone conversations they had got from my landline as evidence against me. Luckily enough, after the conversation with my drug-dealer friend, I was aware and made sure that what they actually picked up from my phone was absolute nonsense and bullshit. They still tried their best to use this evidence against me, but it didn't make a jot of difference.

With the Bradish boys, it was very difficult for the police because the gang were not really enamoured with mobile phones. They saw them simply as tools to be used once or twice and then discarded. None of the gang had a phone registered in their own name; they used anonymous pay-as-you-go handsets. They rarely used landlines and, when they did have occasion to use a phone, they always behaved as if the police were listening and gave nothing away. The gang were seasoned criminals and completely understood how this technology could be dangerous to them.

Another piece of technology commonly used by police in their surveillance operations is tracking devices, which they can place on suspect vehicles. Roberts mentions in his interviews that the practice of the gang was to actively look for these devices before they got into any vehicle and, if one was found, it would be removed and stuck under the wheel arch of a bus or taxi. The gang would have a bit of a belly laugh imagining the police watching the screens and seeing their tracker moving all around London, while they were free to go and commit more robberies. The police called the placing of GPS trackers on suspects, cars as 'slap-and-track' operations, because that is basically what they did. The trackers, usually a small metal box, are magnetic and could be slapped onto a wheel arch or under the car and then the police would be able to track the vehicle from their own vehicles and be aware of every journey their suspect took. According to Vinnie, the amount of GPS trackers found by the gang on their vehicles over the years would have 'filled a small shed.'

Another method used by the police – and, in particular, by the Flying Squad – to follow and observe their suspects was the Budget rental van. Budget was a company that hired out vehicles to the public, usually vans. The Flying Squad had a contract with them that allowed them use of several of these liveried vans, which were quite ubiquitous on most city streets. Unfortunately for the Flying Squad, somebody in the company spoke to somebody in the criminal world and their cover was blown. By the mid-1990s, any blagger who spotted a Budget rental van in his rear-view mirror, or parked up where a bit of work was to take place, knew it was time to abandon ship and come back another day. There was even a case where a Budget rental van was petrol bombed by a couple of young robbers in east London because they thought it had been planted on the plot by the Flying Squad. It turned out that the van had been hired by a family for a house move. The Flying Squad also had their own black London taxi, which they used to tail suspects and cruise around areas that had been identified as targets for armed robbers.

The trouble for the police in their years-long surveillance of the Bradish gang was that the gang knew most of their tricks, having learned from other criminals and also from watching the TV documentary about the downfall of their one-time leader, 'Gentleman' Jimmy Doyle. That documentary turned out to be a mine of information, not only to the Bradish gang but also to armed robbers everywhere. For the first time, the villains were able to see in full colour exactly how the other side worked and adjust their habits accordingly.

Surveillance by the police does not only involve following criminals but also taking photographs and videoing their daily behaviour. Police also have a tendency to set up Ops, usually in a building close to the suspects' home or in an area that they think might be a target, in order to keep a watch on the daily coming and goings of their suspect. An OP can be anywhere that gives the police a good view of their target and, a lot of the time, if available, the OP will be set up in an abandoned building or an empty house or flat. But if none of these is available, it is quite common for the police to put their OP in occupied houses or office buildings.

Obviously, there is a risk involved in this and any occupied spot has to be seriously researched before approach. Sometimes, as in the case mentioned earlier of Dave Croke, the Armaguard robber, the upstairs of a pub can be used if the publican is sympathetic to the police, but even this can have its dangers. When Croke and Barret had Shield Security Depot in Battersea in their robbing sights, the police plotted up their OP in a pub just across the railway line from the depot. Unfortunately for the publican, when the Croke firm was eventually nicked,

Crimewatch UK did a special on the case and happened to show footage of the Flying Squad in this particular pub. The pub was located on the Patmore estate, which, at that time, was notorious for the amount of young criminals who hung around there. On the evening that the documentary was aired, several young men who had seen their local pub being used by Old Bill marched on the pub and put through all of the windows. They classed this as 'street justice'. The outside of the pub was also spray-painted with the word 'grass' in 2-foot-high letters.

CHAPTER TWENTY-FIVE

ROBBING THE BLIND

On the morning of 20 October 2000, Sean Bradish decided that it was time to rob the security van that Stephen Roberts had been so enthusiastic about for so long. The van was making a pick-up from the RNIB in Alperton, north-west London. The RNIB building was on the sharp corner of a street, which meant the security van could pull up on either side of the building. The van was, according to Roberts, due to arrive at 11am.

Sean was a little bit uneasy that Roberts had done a recce and put the job forward himself and then changed his mind about actually doing it. Roberts had never turned down a job before. He loved the money too much and Sean was wondering if he was losing his bottle. Roberts had told Sean after the robbery in Woodford, where he had held the two police officers at gunpoint, that he was thinking of 'giving the game up', but Sean knew that he was a greedy, ruthless bastard and thought he may just be having a rest. He certainly had no idea that this would be the gang's last job.

The RNIB job had been on the gang's radar since Roberts had first suggested it. He claimed that he had watched the job on several occasions and that the security was crap around the pick-up, and that it seemed as though there was plenty of cash being moved here, as he said they were moving 'ton boxes', which were insured for £100,000. Roberts had certainly talked this job up and now Sean was eager to do it.

A couple of weeks before the job, Sean had picked the team who would be involved. Roberts former best friend (they had fallen out at this time), Steven Wall, was to be on recce, along with Tony Hall. Rob Mason was the designated getaway driver as he was, supposedly, a staunch man and a good and steady driver. Vinnie would also have been on the RNIB job, but he was having a holiday in Ireland at the time. Plus, he was not happy about the job and had warned Sean that it could be a set-up. Sean shrugged. He had no doubt that, if this job was a set-up by police and persons unknown, he would have the intelligence and strength to come out of it untouched.

By this time, Sean's confidence in his own abilities was high; he really believed he was charmed because of all the lucky escapes he'd had. Vinnie no longer trusted Stephen Roberts and made it plain to Sean that the fact Roberts was not going on the job was highly suspicious. He told Sean, 'I wouldn't even take a free lollipop from Roberts. He's not to be trusted.' But Vinnie flew off to

Ireland and Sean decided to ignore his advice. He was thinking about the mega pay-out.

The week before the robbery was due to happen, Sean sent Steven Wall and Tony Hall down to Alperton to watch the movements of the van and check out the area. The two men borrowed a legal car from another friend and headed for the RNIB. They got there around half an hour before the van was scheduled to arrive and found a parking spot from where they could watch the target. Alperton is quite a busy part of north-west London and the two men felt a bit suspicious-looking just hanging around. Perhaps, with hindsight, sending Hall and Wall to do the recce wasn't such a good idea. Both men were nervous and not very experienced in the game, although Sean had thought that, being professional criminals, they would have no trouble spotting any undercover police activity around the plot. Also, he thought, how hard could it be to keep an eye open for a possible ambush and report on whether the van was on time or not?

In the event, it was all academic anyway, as the robbers found out when they were arrested that the Flying Squad had received a tip-off that the Bradish gang was to rob the security van at the RNIB, and already had the target under covert surveillance. Just how the Flying Squad had found out about the job is a mystery. Vinnie Bradish has long been convinced that Stephen Roberts was working directly with the police by this time, and that it was he who set the boys up to be nicked. As the Bradish brothers really kept things close to their chest on jobs like these, it is difficult to say with any certainty exactly how the Flying Squad got their information. Wall, Hall and Mason did not even know about the job until the week before when Sean sent two of them to look at the job and, by that time, the police had already set up an OP and planned their ambush. If it was not Roberts who gave this job to the Flying Squad, that only left Sean and Vinnie Bradish who knew about it in advance, and you can bet the house that neither of them tipped off the police.

Anyway, Hall and Wall watched as the security van pulled up outside the RNIB building. They watched a guard get out and go into the building, and marked the time as 11.15pm. Wall drove towards the security van and Tony Hall gave it a last good, long, hard look. Little did the men know that, right across the street, two Flying Squad officers were videoing them from the top floor of a building where they had set up their OP. This video would later be produced in court as evidence. Another thing that Sean did not find out until he was arrested and given the evidence was that the police had been plotted up on this job since day one. In court, they also produced a video of Sean and Stephen Roberts checking out the same job soon after Roberts had suggested it. That means that either the Flying Squad had solid intel or they sat watching that security van delivery every Thursday for seven weeks!

Steven Wall and Tony Hall met up with Sean after their recce and told him that everything seemed to be 'sweet' at Alperton. They had seen no police and the van had turned up on time and was ripe for picking. Sean decided that the gang would hit it the following week.

With Roberts laying low, Sean had to pay one of the local tearaways to steal him a car for the job. He ended up with a fairly new BMW and was happy with it. In his mind, he figured that this kid could become their new supplier of vehicles if Roberts was taking a rest.

On the morning of 20 October 2000, Sean Bradish, Steven Hall, Tony Wall and Rob Mason set out to rob the RNIB van. Mason joked that they would go down in history as proper monsters, as they were 'robbing the blind.' Wall explained to him that they were not actually robbing blind people and that saying shit like that could jinx them. Sean, from the front passenger seat of the car, told them to 'shut the fuck up and concentrate on keeping your eyes open.'

Rob Mason parked the stolen and plated BMW on a small side street very close to the RNIB building, and Sean took a holdall from the boot of the car and distributed weapons. Mason had nothing, as he would not be leaving the getaway vehicle. Sean had a double-barrelled, sawn-off, 12-gauge shotgun, loaded; Tony Hall had a .22 pistol; and Steven Wall was carrying a Smith & Wesson .38 revolver. Their plan was to approach the guard from different directions in case he tried to get away. They had to get him on the pavement with the box in hand. The gang waited in the car for about ten minutes and then Sean decided that four strange heads parked up in a car looked way too suspicious, so he ordered Hall and Wall out and he got out himself. The robbers split up and just casually walked around the area, looking in shop windows but not straying too far from where the van would park. It was a cold morning and Sean was wearing a blue puffer jacket. He kept his hands deep in his pockets and gripped the shotgun that was hidden under his jacket.

By 11.30pm, the van had still not arrived and the robbers were getting a bit jittery from hanging around the area. It was not unheard of for a security van to be delayed in traffic and turn up late, so robbers were always prepared for that. But Sean started to get a tingle in his spine, which usually warned him that something was not quite right. He started to scan the high windows of the surrounding buildings and, for a second, he thought he saw a reflective flash at one of the windows. This was enough for Sean. He started thinking about the conversation he'd had with Vinnie about the job being a set-up. He was constantly scanning the windows and street for anything suspicious. At 11.45pm, the van still had not put in an appearance and Sean had had enough. He signalled for the other two to head back to the getaway car. This was turning into a bit of a circus and Sean did not want to be the one left wearing the clown make-up. All three robbers got back to the car and climbed in, resigned to missing a big payday but also slightly relieved to be getting out of the area.

Just as Sean climbed into the front passenger seat of the BMW, the street suddenly erupted into action. Three unmarked police vehicles zoomed in to where the BMW was parked and policeman with high-visibility police caps, bulletproof vests and Heckler & Koch sub-machine guns disgorged from the vehicles, shouting commands at the men in the BMW: 'Armed police! Armed police!' 'One officer ran to the front of the car and fired a round into each of the front tyres of the would-be getaway vehicle, to slow it down in case it managed to escape the ambush. And suddenly, the whole street was alive with armed police. They surrounded the car, guns trained on the occupants, they ordered them to drop their weapons.

Sean gripped his shotgun and, at first, fleetingly thought about jumping out of the car and opening fire on the police. But he realised there were way too many of them and they'd already had the element of surprise on their side. Rob Mason was panicking in the driver's seat. When the cop fired at the tyres, he thought he was being fired on and quickly put up his hands so fast he almost broke a finger when he hit the roof of the car. Steven Wall quickly rolled out of the car and threw himself face-down on the road, shouting, 'Don't shoot! Don't shoot! I'm not armed!'

One police officer extended an ASP baton and started smashing the windows on the car. This was done to distract the robbers and give his colleagues a chance to drag them from the vehicle. Within a minute of the initial attack, all four would-be robbers were laying on the road, face-down, as the police plasti-cuffed their wrists.

'Sean Bradish, you are under arrest for conspiracy to rob...'

And that was it. Sean's world had ended with a bang

and not a whimper, unless you counted the whinging coming from Rob Mason as he attempted to tell the Flying Squad officers that they were making a mistake and that he was no more than a cab driver who had been hoodwinked by bad men.

The gang were loaded separately into different police vehicles. The days of the Dirty Dozen were coming to an end.

Two weeks later, on 1 November 2000, the police attended the home of Stephen Roberts. The initial arrest was for robbery and the police had DNA evidence. Roberts had left behind a white baseball cap when he and Sean Bradish had robbed Barclays Bank in Sudbury on Monday, 3 July 2000. This was the robbery in which they had been surprised by CID officers and Robertsit had them at gunpoint. The police knew that DNA evidence was golden and that they would have little trouble getting a conviction on Roberts. As a bonus, a sawn-off shotgun and ammunition was found in the house and Roberts was arrested for possession of firearms and conspiracy to rob. The finding of a loaded shotgun in the home of Roberts kind of gives the lie to his claims to police and courts that he had 'retired' from the gang.

In his first interviews, Roberts said nothing to incriminate anyone. It is only when he was remanded in custody at HMP Wormwood Scrubs that he had a serious change of mind. He claims that it was when he found out that Sean Bradish blamed him for his arrest on the RNIB security-van job and was planning to have him killed. Deep down, he was terrified of Sean Bradish and thought the man was paranoid. But, in the recesses of his crafty and febrile criminal mind, he had been developing a plan; a 'final solution' that he was now ready to put into action. Stephen John Roberts planned to be first man into the lifeboat. Forget women and children first – it was going to be every man for himself.

CHAPTER TWENTY-SIX

PRISON

The prison transport, escorted by vehicles packed with heavily armed police officers, pulled into the service road leading to the gates of Belmarsh prison in Woolwich, south-east London. HMP Belmarsh is a Category A men's prison, which opened in 1991. It holds around a thousand men, of both security Categories A and B. These are mainly remands but the prison also holds convicted and sentenced prisoners awaiting transfer. It is used for high-profile cases, particularly those concerning national security. There are four residential wings, known as houseblocks. In 2000, when the Dirty Dozen gang were being held there, houseblock four was used to hold Category A prisoners. The prison also has a Special Secure Unit (SSU), which is basically a top-security prison within a top-security prison, which houses some of the most dangerous prisoners in the UK.

Sean Bradish was designated as a Category A prisoner

right from the start. The attempted robbery of a security van was a serious charge and the police were not taking any chances with him. His every move would be watched, every word written down in the small blue Category A book that had to accompany him everywhere he went. In order to move anywhere off his own spur of cells on houseblock four, Sean had to be accompanied by at least three prison staff: one to carry his Category A book, one to watch him closely and another with a large Alsatian dog on a short leash. Should Sean Bradish make any sudden moves, all hell would immediately break loose. The staff were very well versed in keeping their high-security prisoners under close watch at all times.

Belmarsh was a prison with a reputation for security and no one had ever escaped from in its twenty-three-year history. The wall itself is 25 feet tall, which includes an anti-grapple dome that covers the top of the entire outer wall. The dome is designed to make it impossible to throw up a hook or grapple in order to scale the wall, as there is no grip on the smooth planes of the dome. Inside the perimeter wall are 20-foot fences made from green-coloured, high-tension wire. Each fence is topped with coils of brutal razor wire that would rip a person to shreds if they tried to cross it. There are myriad CCTV cameras placed strategically all over the entire prison, both inside and out. Each cell has a steel door on a swing hinge, meaning that, even if a prisoner were to try barricading himself inside the polarity of the door can be reversed so that it opens outwards as well as inwards. The small windows of the cells are guarded by manganese steel bars, cut-resistant metal and a steel grille.

In order to get to the SSU from reception, visitors are placed in the back of a windowless van and driven around inside the prison until they can no longer get their bearings before being delivered to the SSU itself. This is so that, if anyone plans on giving an SSU prisoner any information to aid an escape, they will have seen no landmarks to identify and will not even be sure which direction they have come from. Belmarsh is a veritable fortress.

Once inside the Reception compound, Sean Bradish was kept inside the small, featureless cell inside the prison transport for around ten minutes, so that the senior escorting police officer could hand over all the info on Sean to the reception officers. Eventually, the prison staff came to take him off the van. Of course, there was a security routine for this. First, the cell door was unlocked and opened just wide enough for Sean to put both hands through the gap. The screws slipped a pair of heavy-duty prison handcuffs around his wrists and one gripped the middle chain connecting the two cuffs and held it firmly. The cell door was then swung open and the prisoner was pulled out of the cell by the cuffs.

Sean Bradish was no stranger to prison, and he showed no emotion as he was led by the handcuff chain past grim-faced screws and into the prison reception. He was asked his name. He stared at the reception officer for a second. Now was the time to put his marker down and let the screws know that he was no first-timer and no mug to be intimidated by an official show of strength. Start as you mean to go on. 'Don't act the cunt,' he said firmly to the reception officer. 'My name is on nearly every fucking page of that file you've just been handed.'

There was a moment of silence and the six prison officers present waited for the reception officer to reply. He was an experienced senior officer and judged that Sean would probably not go quietly if challenged physically. He had enough staff at his disposal to crush almost any attempt by Sean at getting physical, but he preferred a quiet life. He swallowed Sean's insult and shook his head, sadly. 'No need for the attitude, lad,' he said. 'We're not the police. We're just holding you until your trial, so let's slow down and get this routine done.'

Sean relaxed and shrugged. 'Whatever,' he said, casually.

After the reception routine – he had been stripped and searched and every item of his property logged on his reception record – he was put into a holding cell to await escort to the houseblock. In the old days, before all the swingeing cuts to prison budgets, he would have been given a bath or shower on reception to prison and, after two days in a dirty police-station cell, he could have done with one. He waited, slightly impatiently, for them to decide where he was going to be housed.

After about half an hour, three prison officers, one with the obligatory Alsatian, opened the door of the holding cell and indicated that it was time to move. As he was walked through the back of reception, he passed about twenty prisoners who had just arrived at the prison and were being held in a large holding cell. These were

Category B remand prisoners, sent to prison by the courts with no bail in order to wait for a trial or a hearing. One of the guys in the holding cage called out to Sean. Sean recognised him as one of the hangers-on from the manor, so he nodded in his direction. As a Category A prisoner, he would be ensconced on houseblock four with mostly other Category A men and would not really get a chance to talk to any of the Category B prisoners. Sean knew that he was on his own.

Once on houseblock four, Sean was marked onto the Catagory A board in the small central office before he was shown on to the spur that was to be his home for the next few months.

The cells in Belmarsh are modern and spartan. There was a metal-framed bed bolted to the floor, an MDF cupboard bolted to the wall, a chair and a toilet. The one window was heavily barred and looked out onto a patch of concrete exercise yard. Each of the spurs on houseblock four featured CCTV on each landing. The spur held seventy prisoners, over two-thirds of whom were Category A and the rest high-risk Category B. Everyone on the spur was on remand, awaiting trial and sentence. Sean settled in and awaited his deposition bundle: the paperwork, statements and photographs that the prosecution would use in order to get a conviction. He was smart enough to know that, by studying the depositions, he might spot some mistake that he could use to bolster his own case.

At this stage, Sean had little idea that his old blagging partner, Stephen Roberts, was already singing like the proverbial canary. Sean did not know that, even as he paced his small top-security cell in Belmarsh prison, trying to spot a way out of the RNIB robbery, Roberts was opening a much bigger can of worms. Pretty soon it would feel as though his life was circling a drain, just waiting to be sucked in. And if he thought the security around him couldn't get any tighter, he would soon be in for a rude awakening.

CHAPTER TWENTY-SEVEN

MORE TROUBLE

Sean Bradish was being held in the SSU at Belmarsh prison. A veritable fortress right in the centre of the prison and known as the prison within a prison. He had been there since just after his arrest on 20 October 2000, and was charged with conspiracy to rob the security van at the RNIB and possession of a firearm. Even though he had been isolated in the SSU, he had been hearing, via phone calls home, that Stephen Roberts had been arrested and was now spilling his guts all over the police-station floor, so he was expecting a visit from the police to talk about Roberts's revelations. Sean was not too worried, as he figured the game wasn't over until the judge gave the final nod. It would be his word against Roberts, and Sean knew that he had more than a fighting chance as long as he didn't give up hope.

Sure enough, at around 9am on Monday, 5 February 2001, his cell door was thrown open and he was told that the police were waiting for him. He was taken to the office of the SSU, where three Flying Squad officers – DS Willerton, DC Thurlow and DC Warlow – stood, looking pretty pleased with themselves. Sean looked at them and waited.

Sergeant Willerton stepped forward and gave Sean the bad news. 'Sean Bradish, there have been further developments in our investigation so you will now be transferred to Colindale Police Station, where you will be detained for a court-ordered period not exceeding five days.' The police had to get special dispensation for holding Sean over the standard police custody time of twenty-four hours.

At 11.15am, after a break-neck, siren-blaring drive through London, the Flying Squad vehicle pulled into the yard at Colindale Police Station and Sean was escorted into the custody suite. DS Willerton then informed Sean that he was being further arrested for forty-one other offences, incorporating thirty-eight armed robberies, two assaults and the attempted murder of a police officer. Sean was cautioned and Willerton asked him if he understood. Impassive as ever, Sean nodded his head.

Once he had been told the bare bones of the charges the police were hoping to lay at his door, Sean was locked in a cell to think about them while the police prepared for their interrogation.

It is pretty standard practice to keep a suspect in suspense at police stations. The police will put you in a cell and leave you there for hours on end until they are ready to interview. Psychologically, the time spent locked in the cell is supposed to soften you up in preparation for the interview – to give the suspect time to wallow in his own guilt and misery – but, with Sean, it was just a boring waste of time. Being in a small, airless, windowless cell for the night was not going to kill him; in fact, it was a nice break from the regimented regime in the SSU at Belmarsh. Sean simply read the novel he had brought with him from the prison and then got his head down.

There is a concept among some police detectives that the easiest way to spot a guilty man is to put him into a police cell and observe his behaviour. If he paces the cell, endlessly wringing his hands and looking scared and worried, the odds are good that he is innocent. If, on the other hand, the suspect immediately gets his head down and looks bored, it is because he is probably guilty. Not an exact science by any stretch of the imagination, but the police were happy to see Sean sleeping in his cell.

The next day – 6 February 2001 – Sean was taken out of his cell for a series of police interviews concerning the new charges that Roberts had brought into the light. Sean had four police interviews on that day and had decided from the start that he was not going to co-operate. In each interview, Sean moved his chair so that he could sit with his back to the interrogation team and remained silent throughout, refusing to answer even to his name. His attitude was, 'If you've got all this so-called evidence, charge me and let's get it on. Let the jury sort it out.'

The police realised they were getting nothing from Sean, and they hadn't really expected a tsunami of co-operation from this man, whom they considered a hardened and dedicated professional criminal. The last interview was finished by 3.07pm and the police decided there was no value in trying to interview their silent witness any further, as the only sound in the interview room all day had been police asking the questions. At 4.08pm, Sean was taken from his cell to the custody desk of the station and was charged and cautioned, to which he spoke his only words in that police station: 'I am not guilty of any of those offences.' That evening, Sean was returned to the SSU at Belmarsh prison under armed guard.

CHAPTER TWENTY-EIGHT

THE ARREST OF VINCENT BRADISH

By February 2001, Vinnie Bradish was the only main player still left outside prison. Sean was a double-Category A prisoner in the SSU in HMP Belmarsh, looking down the wrong end of a twenty-year sentence; Roberts was tucked up in a luxury supergrass cell in Paddington Police Station, singing his treacherous heart out; and the minor players, with a couple of exceptions, were remanded in HMP Wormwood Scrubs.

The police had been hot on Vinnie's trail since the rest of the gang had been mopped up and he had been lying low, staying at a different place every night and expecting the door to come through at any moment. At this time, Vinnie didn't exactly know what Roberts had told the police but, when people all over the manor started getting lifted, he knew it was not good as far as he was concerned. The relationship between Vinnie and Roberts had never been great. Vinnie had accepted him simply because Sean had, so he knew that, if the shit hit the fan, Roberts was going to do his best to make sure Vinnie got heavily splashed.

On Monday, 26 February 2001, Vinnie decided to go back to Wembley to visit a relative. He was driving a green Jaguar with a woman in the passenger seat and, as he turned into Beresford Road, NW4, he glanced in his rear-view mirror and spotted a suspicious-looking car on his tail. He saw that there were at least three bodies in the car and that got his nerves jangling. He wasn't armed and he wasn't so good a driver that he would be able to outmanoeuvre highly trained Flying Squad drivers. Then he noticed another sussy-looking vehicle behind the first one and he knew he was caught bang to rights. He decided that his only course of action was to brace himself for a pull.

The statement of DC Kym Brain, which she read out in court, tells exactly what happened next. Kym and other officers from the Flying Squad, DC Harris, DS Dower and PC Borlase, were on duty in an unmarked police vehicle. Kym and DS Dower were both armed with Glock service-issue police pistols. As the group made their way towards Beresford Avenue, in Wembley, in the direction of the North Circular, they spied a green Jaguar car, being tailed by another Flying Squad vehicle. Kym recalls:

> I heard the instruction for the vehicle to be stopped, via the radio. The lead police vehicle pulled alongside the Jaguar and we took up a position behind the

Jaguar. I saw the Jaguar collide with a stationary vehicle parked on the near side. I saw that officers had got out of the lead vehicle. I got out of the vehicle I was in. I was wearing a high-visibility police baseball cap. I made my way to the front near-side [passenger] door of the Jaguar where I could see a white female sitting. I drew my handgun and issued the challenge of 'Armed police!' I could hear that other officers who were on the other side of the Jaguar were also issuing the 'Armed police' challenge. I heard glass smashing and more challenges being called.

At this point, Kym recalls seeing DC Harris make his way to the passenger door and tell the female suspect to get out of the car. From Kym's position at the front passenger door, she could see that the man, whom she knew to be Vinnie Bradish, was being pulled out of the driver's seat by other officers and she re-holstered her handgun. Bradish was struggling violently with the officers, who managed to force him to the ground. After the officers got him face-down on the pavement, Kym was able to place handcuffs on him, before she and DC Dunsford searched his clothes for concealed weapons. Once they had cleared Bradish for weapons, the officers administered first aid to his head, which was bleeding – but not before they had arrested and cautioned him for conspiracy to commit armed robberies. Kym remembers, 'He made no reply to my caution at 7.27pm. I said to Bradish, "Are you all right?" I was referring to his head injuries. He said, "That Roberts has been talking a load of shit." I said, "For now, let's sort out your injuries."'

Although trained officers recounting arrests have a tendency to make them sound like dry, mundane affairs, in reality, arrests by armed police officers are hectic, violent and sudden. Vinnie did not just happen to run his Jaguar into a parked car. The Flying Squad vehicle pulled alongside him and deliberately forced him, head-on, to run into the vehicle. There were sixteen police officers involved in Vinnie's arrest, the majority of them armed, so imagine all of those gun-toting coppers swarming the car and smashing the windows through before dragging him onto the pavement. Vinnie says he received the head injuries from being pistol-whipped by one of the squad as they dragged him from the car.

This kind of surprise attack is the stock-in-trade of the Flying Squad. Their aim is to disorientate the person being arrested and make sure that, if they are armed, they will have little time to produce and use a weapon. I suppose it must be expected from a trained squad whose milieu is used to dealing with armed and violent men.

Also, I feel I must mention that age-old police trick of 'verballing' suspects at their arrest. Even if an arrested suspect remains as silent as a lonely grave during his arrest, he will invariably find incriminating utterances supposedly given by him in the notebooks of the arresting officers. In days gone by, the police verbals attributed to criminals were not very sophisticated, usually amounting to something like, '...I then arrested Chummy for armed robbery and he replied, "Oh my gawd, I'm so glad you've nicked me, guv'nor. I was getting out of control and may have shot someone on one of these blags!'" A nice little admission even before a statement has been taken. But, after the highly publicised miscarriage-of-justice cases that finally came to the fore in the late 1980s, juries – and even some judges – were less inclined to believe any old tut that coppers put up as gospel when the only people present were the police and the suspect himself.

The Police And Criminal Evidence (PACE) Act of 1984 put a stop to statements being taken in police cars or cells and made sure that all interviews were taped and videoed. This meant that unscrupulous police officers could no longer beat or threaten statements out of suspects. But the contemporaneous notes at arrest were not covered and verballing carries on right up to the present time.

Perhaps one of the most infamous cases of police verballing involved a young man called Derek Bentley, who was hanged for supposedly killing a police officer during a burglary on a sweet factory in Croydon in 1953. Bentley was already under arrest when his accomplice, Christopher Craig, shot and killed PC Miles. But Craig was only sixteen at the time and too young to hang. Bentley, on the other hand, was nineteen years old and eligible for the drop. Police officers gave evidence that, before Craig shot PC Miles, Derek Bentley had cried out, 'Let him have it, Chris!' Bentley denied he had ever uttered these words, but he was found guilty of murder and hanged for the murder.

On 30 July 1998, Derek Bentley was posthumously granted a pardon, his conviction quashed, and his name cleared. It was forty-five years after they executed him at HMP Wandsworth. It turned out that the same police officer who attributed the fateful words to poor Derek Bentley had attributed the exact same words in evidence to another offender three years before Bentley was even arrested.

Vinnie Bradish also claims that the Flying Squad verballed him during his arrest. According to Vinnie, he stayed silent during his arrest, asking only for his solicitor, but the police thought it might be prudent to establish a link between Bradish and their prized canary, Roberts, right from the start, hence the supposed crack about Roberts. All of the Flying Squad officers present at the arrest of Vincent Bradish marked the exact same verbal mentioning Roberts. But, of course, they would, as they prepared their notes together.

At Colindale Police Station, Vinnie Bradish gave no-comment answers once his legal representative was there. The police outlined their case and told Vinnie some of the things that Roberts had been saying. After two days in the station, Vinnie was charged and cautioned. According to official records, he made no comment and remained silent.

The last of the gang was finally arrested and on his way to HMP Belmarsh. The Flying Squad were as pleased as punch and celebrations were on the cards. With the evidence of Stephen Roberts to put in front of a jury, the squad were optimistic about getting convictions. They had taken one of the most prolific robbery gangs off the streets without a shot being fired. Bad days were coming for the last of the Dirty Dozen.

CHAPTER TWENTY-NINE

'THE FLYING SQUAD SAVED MY LIFE...'

'Sean wasn't satisfied. He took a half-pint glass, smashed it then rammed it in the man's face about 30 times. I had never seen so much blood. We tried to stop him, but he turned on us. He'd become an absolute animal.'

Stephen Roberts interview with the *Observer*

Before disappearing into the ether of a hidden part of the British criminal justice system, Stephen Roberts gave one final interview to the *Observer* newspaper, in which he spoke about his life and his reasons for betraying his former friends. Perhaps the most surprising claim he made was that the Flying Squad 'saved [his] life!'. It seems he was claiming that being arrested and sentenced to a token sentence of eight years had saved him from being shot dead on the street whilst carrying out acts of robbery. He certainly cannot have been talking about his life being in danger from his former partners-in-crime because, until the Flying Squad arrested him, there was no evidence that anyone actually planned to harm him. Certainly, Vinnie Bradish did not like Roberts, but until Roberts began to cough his lot there was no real danger to him.

Roberts was keen to stress that by the time of his arrest he had been trying to distance himself from the gang and had given up going on robberies with them. He claimed he wanted to give up his life of crime and had been looking for a straight job when the police pounced. That might be more believable had he not been found in possession of a sawn-off shotgun when he was arrested. If, as he claims, he was going straight, then why the need for an illegal weapon, the tool of the armed robber?

I think, once again, we have to look at anything Roberts says and take it with a large pinch of salt. Which really does beg the question, why did the police and courts accept his version of events without any other real evidence? As his own comments about robbing drug dealers whilst disguised as a police officer have shown, some of what he has said does invite some scrutiny.

After the trial of the Bradish gang at the Old Bailey, Roberts' life was under threat and he entered the UK version of the witness protection programme. He still had a prison sentence of eight years to serve, but nobody could have been under the illusion that he was going to serve much of that or that he was going to be put out on a normal prison landing like a neon target. Besides the men Roberts betrayed, UK prisons are full of men who would gladly serve an extra prison sentence for a chance to stick a blade into or throw scalding water over a known supergrass. Roberts would have been maimed or murdered in pretty short order. Instead, he would be held on the Bloggs Unit in Parkhurst prison on the Isle of Wight, a unit specially set up to house dealers whilst disguised criminal supergrasses.

Roberts told the *Observer* that his early childhood was happy and that he came from a good, honest family. It was only in his teenage years that he became a criminal. He claims he started in the way that most young criminals and troublemakers do, by hanging out with 'a bad crowd' in Harlesden, and things just deteriorated from there. He talked of first meeting the Bradish brothers in a notorious pub that had become a hangout for serious criminals, and how he had been impressed by their gangster talk and sharp clothes. He, too, wanted the expensive suits, the wads of money and the flash cars, so he did his best to get noticed by the gang.

Drinking in the same pub, Roberts soon became friends with the Bradish boys – Sean in particular. At the time, he was already deep into the criminal world and nursing a growing addiction to Class A drugs. He got involved in his first robbery when Sean, unable to obtain a car for the job, asked Roberts to steal one for him. To Roberts, this was like his dream come true. In his mind he had finally hit the big time and would soon be enjoying the rewards of major crime. Plus, hanging around with seriously violent criminals meant that no one could mess with him. All the dealers who had refused him credit, all the girls who blanked him and all the other people who 'took the piss' would now have to change their tunes and show him some respect. For Stephen Roberts, joining the Dirty Dozen gang was a ticket to riches, respect and a certain type of fame.

Roberts joined the Bradish brothers in robbing a Thomas Cook travel shop and, though pretty nervous at first, he soon started to enjoy the excitement, the rush of adrenalin, that he got from committing armed robberies. His first job with the gang netted £24,000 in cash – more money than Roberts had ever seen in his life. He was hooked.

He loved the routine that the gang had established after each robbery – where they would book into a top hotel to count their ill-gotten gains and then go on spending sprees and wind up in the hotel bar drinking champagne and snorting cocaine until the early hours. Spending £3,000 on a drink-and drug-fuelled weekend was pretty standard for the gang, and Roberts' jumped right into the deep end. And with the money and the kudos, came the women.

And what did he make of Sean Bradish? Roberts claimed that he began to worry that Sean was becoming too violent. He claims that Sean was always going to be prepared to shoot someone if things started going wrong, but looking at the evidence overall it seems to have been Roberts himself who was always the first with threats to kill or kneecap people. It was Roberts who took the shotgun and threatened to blow the heads off two plain clothes officers when they were disturbed during a robbery. It was also Roberts who boasted about robbing drug dealers armed with a machete before he even met the Bradish brothers. And, as Vinnie might remind us, it was Roberts who fired a shotgun in a fit of pique, pointlessly killing a duck. There is little doubt that both Sean and Vinnie Bradish and the other members of the gang were all men for whom instrumental violence came easily, and Roberts was no shrinking wallflower in that gang.

In order to paint Sean Bradish as the most violent member of the gang, Roberts likes to tell of an incident when the gang were drinking in a Harlesden pub when a man suspected of rape came in. He claims that the man was taken outside and given a beating by the gang, but that Sean Bradish could not control himself and 'took a half-pint glass, smashed it and then rammed into the man's face about thirty times'. He said that Sean became 'an absolute animal. He was just itching to kill someone, and I didn't want any part of that.'

There is no doubt that Stephen Roberts' drug use was spiralling out of control. He went from spending £25 a night on cocaine, to snorting up a thousand-pounds worth daily. It is quite obvious to anyone with experience of drugs and drug addiction that using such a large amount of cocaine can lead to psychosis, paranoia and erratic behaviour. But, despite the heavy drug use, Roberts told the police and the *Observer* that he had been thinking of going back to laying bricks for a living. Does it seem plausible that someone with a £1,000-per-day drug habit would decide to give up crime? With no attempt at rehab? When he appeared for trial Roberts was faced with one of his ex-girlfriends giving evidence from the witness-box who accused him of lying about the Bradish brothers simply because she'd had an affair with Vinnie Bradish whilst still in a relationship with Roberts. She claimed that Stephen Roberts had gone 'crazy with jealously'. Of course, Roberts claimed she was lying.

It would seem that despite the very obvious discrepancies in his story the police and the jury accepted his version of events. The statement of Stephen Roberts is littered with stories designed to shift the blame for everything from himself onto the Bradish brothers. And, this is not surprising as the evidence of a supergrass will always be designed to minimize and mitigate his own actions whilst setting up others as the real villains.

Roberts had been more than happy to join the Dirty Dozen, despite the fact that he knew they made their living by violent and unlawful means. He was ready, willing and able to pursue financial gain at the point of a gun, to threaten innocents with shooting, and to use the proceeds in pursuit of a very expensive drug habit. Perhaps he did have a change of heart after a few years of enjoying the high life, maybe he genuinely wanted to give up the money, the drugs, the cars and lay bricks for a living. But you have to ask yourself one question – does that seem likely?

CHAPTER THIRTY

AFTERS

On 7 March 2002, Sean Bradish, who by now was already serving a life term for armed robbery on a security van outside the RNIB in Alperton, north-west London, was given four life sentences at the Old Bailey in London for a string of robberies spanning five years and for stealing nearly £250,000. Sean had previously been arrested in October 2000, while Vincent was nicked in January 2001 and sentenced to twenty-two years for his part in the raids after a Flying Squad operation code-named Odie was launched to track them down. The brothers were said in court to resemble the Mitchell brothers from the television series *EastEnders* as the jury heard how they had terrorised bank and travel staff and robbed security vans at gunpoint to finance a life of luxury. But the pair were eventually caught when their fellow gang-member-turned-supergrass, Steven Roberts, implicated them in at least fifty robberies between 1995 and 2000. From those raids, officers then picked twenty-four where they had corroborative evidence to form the basis of conspiracy charges. Looking back now, Vincent remarks:

You could see that Roberts was sneaky looking. He was always very paranoid and looking over his shoulder – even when we went out to the pub. When we were arrested for the robberies and I read the interviews, you could see why he was so paranoid because it looked like he'd been setting up everyone for years – drug dealers, for example. He'd be buying drugs and the next thing the dealers would get raided. So, obviously, he's grassed them up. He's put the police onto them. He'd be getting firearms off of people and he'd be probably be doing the same. And selling firearms to people and they'd then get raided. So he'd been setting people up for years and he admitted it all in his interviews. He admits to buying drugs off of this one, setting up that one, impersonating the police. He admitted aggravated burglary, attempted murder of the police, everything. So he got everything off his chest, so to speak, when he was arrested, and that was that.

Asked if he could ever return to a life of crime, Vincent laments:

No, not really. I couldn't see it. I just got sick of it in the end. Even before I was nicked, I was getting bored with some of the robberies. I wasn't doing anything with the money. You were just squandering it all and I wasn't getting enough to buy myself a nice house. If I had got, like, a hundred grand and I could put twenty grand down here... I wasn't getting no financial advice. I wouldn't say I was getting sick of it. I was getting sick of doing small jobs. I wanted to do bigger jobs. I wanted to do a cash depot because that's where all the money is, ain't it. [Laughing.] We didn't make it to the cash depot. That's like the top of the mountain. Like, for me, that would've been the peak. I know people that have done cash depots and got away with it. They'd get away with a couple of million. Sometimes they would crash through the walls and sometimes coming down through the ceiling on a rope – some James Bond type of shit. There'd be good planning going into that and I'm sure, if I'd have met up with some of these people before we got nicked, I would've joined up with them doing that stuff as well.

Was it all worth it? 'Sometimes, when I think about it – yeah,' Vincent reflects:

I had a good time when I was doing it. I was able to do what I wanted with my life. I was enjoying my life. I wasn't having to get up for work at five or six o'clock in the morning. I was getting up at ten o'clock, eleven o'clock, and I could do what I wanted – go to the gym, buy nice clothes. I could do everything. I was living like a millionaire and buying whatever I wanted so I was happy, but it was never enough. I always wanted more, you know. I always wanted to make more money out of it.

But could Bradish have made the same amount of money doing a regular job?

I would never have made the money that I made doing a regular job. We used to talk about that. We'd say, never in a million years, if you lived to be a hundred, you wouldn't have been able to make that money. And even if you're working, your money goes straight into the bank and you'd never even get to see it. We'd have bundles of it, and we could spend it as we pleased. Sometimes you're getting between twenty grand, or a hundred grand if we robbed a bank or a Thomas Cook, and it might only take twenty or thirty seconds. We couldn't say, 'How is that not worth it?' We'd say, 'Of course it's worth it.'

But then, when you'd go to prison, the thing you'd miss the most is your family. That's what makes the prison time hard – missing your loved ones outside. You miss your kids growing up, so to say, Is it worth it?' – it's not worth it in the sense that you miss your kids growing up and you miss your nephews and nieces and all your family growing up and sharing that part of their life with them. As you get older – and I see myself now at fifty-four – the family, they're all doing their own thing and they've got their own kids, whereas, when we were all younger, you were all together more so you're sharing that time together. You miss all that time – you can't get it back. You do ten or twelve years in the nick, you come out, people have moved on, your family's moved on. They're living at different sides of London, you don't hardly see each other.

So, is it worth it? It's a hard one to say. Sometimes you're so skint you start doing these things and you do the robberies. But for things that you miss out on, when you look at it that way, you say no, nothing's worth it because you'd have liked to have been there with my son when he was growing up, but there's nothing you can do about it now, is there? The last bit of bird that I done, that was the longest that I'd served. I did ten years, then I got released. I went out and had a few drinks and, when I got back to the prison, they breathalysed me and I got sent back to closed conditions for nearly another two years. So that was nearly twelve years altogether. The shortest sentence that I served was three months.

In February 2014, Sean Patrick Bradish, who was coming to the end of serving four life sentences, was given three life sentences at the Old Bailey after carrying out a string of armed robberies while on day release from jail. Sean, on release from HMP Spring Hill with an address in Shoot Up Hill in Kilburn, would now have to serve at least eight and a half years before being considered for parole. Among other offences, he pleaded guilty to six counts of robbery and two counts of attempted robbery after stealing an estimated £43,000. He also admitted nine counts of possession of an imitation firearm with intent to cause fear of violence.

The raids took place all across London, from April 2012 until March 2014, the first being when Sean walked into a Lloyds TSB on Finchley Road and threatened staff, who swiftly handed over £8,500. In September that same year, he escaped with £6,500 after carrying out a similar raid at the same bank on Finchley Road. Giving evidence about the raid, a witness said she was grabbed by Bradish, who held a gun to her head while one cashier gasped, 'You're kidding me,' when he robbed her for a third time.

In an attempt to capture the robber, detectives launched Operation Huvadu and Sean was eventually arrested in Northwood, Middlesex, after committing another offence in Uxbridge. Detectives looking into the raids discovered Sean had been captured on CCTV a month before at a clothes shop in Kilburn, buying a blue coat and trainers, which were identical to clothing worn by a robber in Cricklewood. The silver imitation gun, which he had used for four of the raids, was never found. Speaking after the hearing, Detective Sergeant Ben Kennedy of the Flying Squad concluded: 'Bradish's offending escalated over a period of eleven months, with him becoming more brazen as time went on. Bradish showed blatant disregard for the restrictions imposed on him and, had he not been caught when he did, I have no doubt he would have carried on offending. A number of the victims caught up in the robberies genuinely feared for their lives and are still coming to terms with their terrifying ordeals. I hope that they, too, find comfort in today's sentence.'

The Bradish Clan have had more than their fair share of tragedy over the years. Vincent describes the pain of losing his two brothers and young nephew:

Coleman, he was thirty-two and he died of cancer of the liver, and then, a year later, in 1996, my brother Francis died in a car crash. He was in the passenger seat of his own car but the fella he was with was speeding and they had a head-on collision in Adelaide Road, Chalk Farm. The driver survived but my brother Francis died. He was in the passenger seat and the three girls in the back, they all suffered bad injuries. As soon as one of the girls came out of her coma in the hospital, she asked where my brother Francis was. We didn't want to say that he was already gone, in case it sent her back into a coma. We said, 'He's fine, he's fine, don't worry.' And she said, 'He was just sitting here a minute ago and he told me everything's gonna be OK.' For me, I think Francis helped bring her out of the coma, you know. He's told her everything's gonna be OK. And that was that.

The year before Coleman died, my six-year-old nephew died of meningitis. So, when them three deaths happened, one after the other, I just went more and more off the rails then – we were just going on the piss, drinking all the time to get over the deaths. I was robbing all around me. I didn't care less about anything, whether I lived or died. We were just going wild. I used to say, 'I don't give a fuck.' You're just drinking yourself to death and ruining your health, you know.

More heartbreaking news hit the family when Sean's son, twenty-one-year-old Josh Hanson, was stabbed to death in an unprovoked attack in a bar in Eastcote, west London, in 2015. An international manhunt was launched to find the killer, thirty-year-old Shane O'Brien from Ladbroke Grove, west London. After widespread media coverage of the case, O'Brien was arrested in Romania, extradited and convicted at the Old Bailey after three and a half years on the run. 'Josh had just been up to see Sean that day in prison,' Vincent explains. 'That was the last time my brother seen him, so again, that was bad for the whole family.

Now firmly on the straight and narrow, Vincent Bradish avoids the old pitfalls of the past by staying busy.

I'm working now, doing carpentry. I've been doing that since I came out of prison five years ago. I did carpentry work before I went away but I never stuck at it. This is the longest that I've worked now for five years. I retired when I left school, I think. I've only just started working. I like Cuban salsa dancing too. I overheard the Latin music playing in The Crown in Cricklewood when I was walking through the foyer, funnily enough. I went upstairs to investigate, and I see everyone dancing, smiling and happy. I decided then that I had to learn it. Even when I told them I had just got out of prison, they helped me out a lot. I had no money when I wasn't working but they said, 'Don't stop the lessons. We'll give you them for free.' I respected that, you know what I mean? It keeps me away from all the pub life because now I'm going out to salsa clubs. There's nice people there and it's a completely different environment. I go out and I don't even drink sometimes, and I have a great night just dancing away.

So take note, all you Salsa lovers out there: the next time you're invited onto the dance floor, you may well find yourself in the arms of one of the Dirty Dozen.

POSTSCRIPT

I have to admit that I have been an armed robber myself and have taken part in scores of armed robberies over a thirty-year career. I have also served the prison time for my crimes and changed my ways. It was a personal tragedy that led to me seeking rehabilitation for myself. In the cases of the men described in this book, Sean Bradish has not 'officially' finished his sentence, which started in the year 2000. Due to his antics on day release, Sean remains a top-security prisoner with no sniff of the gate for many more years. Vincent 'Vinnie' Bradish served his sentence for the Dirty Dozen robberies and decided that prison and criminal offending were no longer for him. Vinnie has been rehabilitated and is no longer involved in crime. The rest of the gang are either dead, in prison or, in the case of Stephen Roberts, living under an assumed name.

Let us be in no doubt, armed robbery is a serious

and dangerous crime, which leaves in its wake many traumatised victims. Some people may casually shrug at this but think for a moment what your attitude would be if it was your wife, mother, son or husband who was grabbed around the neck and had a loaded gun pointed at their face. How would you feel if one of your relatives was a cashier or a cash-in-transit guard having to face the guns and growls of gangs like the Dirty Dozen? I guess it would then feel very far from being a caper or an exciting episode. Even the people who are not physically harmed during an armed robbery can still suffer a degree of deep trauma. Imagine you are quietly going about your day, minding your own business, and then, through no fault of your own, you are confronted by armed and masked men who threaten to do you harm. Some people cannot just shrug this sort of thing off – it can be mentally and emotionally damaging to the victims. It can lead to years of mental and emotional trauma and can, in some cases, ruin lives.

When I decided to change my life – to stop being a professional criminal/prisoner – it was a long and hard road. I spent five years in a therapeutic prison, undertaking psychodrama sessions and daily group therapy in order to understand how my life had come to such a state. I had lived the same kind of lives as Jimmy Doyle, Sean Bradish, Vinnie Bradish and Stephen Roberts; I had grown up in poverty as a second-generation Irish immigrant and I, too, had taken to crime at an early age. I ended up landing in over forty prisons over the years and it was in these places that I mixed with other major criminals like the ones in this book. But the difference was that I wanted out and was determined to put the violence, prison and crime behind me. Some people – in truth, the majority – who get involved in serious crime from a young age are never given the opportunity to change their lives for the better. You would think that, as a minimum, some probation officer, prison officer or someone in authority would make it their job to intervene at an early stage of a young criminal's career and spell out exactly what will happen to them if they carry on with a criminal lifestyle but, from my own experience, nobody ever does. The system seems to now take it for granted that young criminals are confirmed criminals and should be treated as such.

Of course, these days, we have had successive governments whose big plan to tackle offending and re-offending is to build more prisons. This fills me with despair. It is almost like they are investing in the future criminality of our children. If you build them, you will fill them – it is as simple as that. The more prisons you have, the more prisoners you will have. In my own personal experience, I have come to believe that this country reaches for the prison-stick way too often, and for some really quite petty crimes. For example, as you read these words, there will be an average of between 15,000 and 18,000 people in the British prison system on remand – that is people who have yet to be convicted, let alone sentenced, for any crime. This kind of gives the lie to one of the most oft-repeated proud boasts by politicians and public alike that 'every man is innocent until proven guilty under British law.' Really? Try telling that to the poor saps sharing a cell with two strangers and shitting where they eat in local prisons up and down this country.

There are men, women and children right now in our prisons who are mentally ill or addicted to drink, drugs or gambling – there is no treatment but prison for these people. How can that possibly be right? Of the near 90,000 people in the British prison system, there are probably a maximum of 5,000 who really need to be in prison for the protection of the public. The rest are window dressing; victims of a system that is overlooked by cowardly politicians who jerk their ample knees every time someone from the tabloid media says 'boo!', and a malleable public that is easily frightened and led by the nose.

My point here is not to try to elicit sympathy for serious criminals – after all, they chose their lifestyle and most pursue it with indecent vigour – but to point out that there may be other influences at work here. I would guess that early interventions in the cases of Jimmy Doyle and Sean Bradish would have had little effect on these men. They were single-minded adrenaline junkies who pursued their lives of crime with determination and ruthlessness. But other gang members may have had different lives if one of the many officials who looked at their juvenile offending (they all had previous convictions for petty crime as juveniles) had decided to step in and make an effort to divert them from their unorganised lives of drifting destruction.

But I digress. The fact is that there will always be

young, working-class men with little education but plenty of bottle who will choose professional crime as their career. But I doubt if there will ever be a gang like the Dirty Dozen, who got away with so much for so long.

NOEL 'RAZOR' SMITH, 2020

ACKNOWLEDGEMENTS

I would like to thank my agents, Cat Ledger and Mal Peachy, without whom this book would not be here. And Sophie Hicks for taking over at the last minute. Also, big thanks to Vinnie Bradish for the interviews, Andy Nolan for the interview and all the others who spoke to me but do not want to be named.

Cent
15/09/20